Imaginative CANVAS EMBROIDERY

Imaginative CANVAS EMBROIDERY

Nancy Outram Hobbs

PITMAN PUBLISHING

First published 1976

PITMAN PUBLISHING LTD
Pitman House, Parker Street, Kingsway, London WC2B 5PB
PO Box 46038, Banda Street, Nairobi, Kenya

PITMAN PUBLISHING PTY LTD
Pitman House, 158 Bouverie Street, Carlton, Victoria 3053, Australia

PITMAN PUBLISHING CORPORATION
6 East 43 Street, New York, NY 10017, USA

SIR ISAAC PITMAN (CANADA) LTD
495 Wellington Street West, Toronto, Canada M5V 1G1

THE COPP CLARK PUBLISHING COMPANY
517 Wellington Street West, Toronto, Canada M5V 1G1

ISBN 0 273 00867 6

G62:16

Text set in 12/13pt Photon Imprint, printed by photolithography, and bound in Great Britain at The Pitman Press, Bath

This book is dedicated to Nigel Gow-Smith, Clarence and Mara Outram, Florence and Edwin Ritzheimer and Janice and John Ehrhardt, all of whom have given me encouragement and love during its creation and before.

Many thanks to all the people who so freely contributed their time and talents to help me write this book, especially:

Rosie Hunter, David Lewis, Mavis McDonald, Hugh Russell, Chris Russell, Edward Reynolds, Jean Evans, Theo Lewis, Hilda Sale, David Sale, Anne French, Bernard Berthon, Heather Clark, Jean Carter and her students, Joanne Graham, Mrs Howard Jones, Anne Warren, and Wendy McKie and her students.

I greatly appreciated the co-operation of the staff of the Embroiderers' Guild; Luxury Needlepoint, 36 Beauchamp Place, London SW3; the British Crafts Centre; and Haandarbejdets Fremme (Danish Handicraft Guild), Vimmelskaftet 38, 1161 Copenhagen K., Denmark.

Contents

Introduction

If you are the kind of person who enthusiastically embraces the idea of creating something with your hands, canvas embroidery is a craft that may well entrance. It is difficult not to be absorbed by the delights of this relaxing art form.

There are many reasons why canvas embroidery is so engaging; one of them is the materials, especially the wool. Being a natural fibre, wool has a very particular quality; a manufactured product cannot quite match it. It has warmth and softness, both to the eye and to the touch. It dyes beautifully to many different shades and colours, and is long-lasting and versatile.

Wool, needles, canvas and stitches together make an excellent medium for expressing your creativity. There are so many different directions you can take—learning the stitches, creating new ones and altering the old; experimenting with colours, abstracts and figures in designs; adapting other people's designs or sketching your own as well as stitching the pieces and thinking of new ways to use them.

Canvas embroidery is a craft that is easily mastered. Once you begin a project, you can take it with you anywhere. You can pick it up and stitch for a few minutes or spend an entire evening, and one of its most rewarding qualities is that no matter how many or how few stitches you work in one sitting, you will always see progress and change in your canvas.

In writing this book, I have tried to anticipate the reader's questions and write concise and informative instructions. Needlework experts all have their own theories of the best way to teach canvas-embroidery stitches. Some say that a clear diagram is best, scorning written instructions as cumbersome. I believe that written instructions are as necessary as a diagram and should not be omitted. Too often what is a clear, straightforward diagram to an expert embroiderer is unclear to someone who has never worked the stitch before. Occasionally, through their inexperience, beginners find a stitch simply impossible to work and give up in frustration. By including a diagram with the written instructions, I feel you should have no difficulty in understanding how to work the stitches.

I have also tried to suggest some new ideas for projects. Using a traditional craft in innovative ways can only help to maintain the interest in its revival. Hopefully, some of the suggestions presented here will encourage you to explore your own thoughts, experiment with your own ideas, and thus to contribute to the revival. At the very least, whatever you make, you will have the satisfaction of knowing that you have taught yourself to work the stitches; I find there are few more satisfying and exciting experiences in our mechanized society.

Finally, I hope you use this book as a workbook because this is what I have tried to make it. I have thought of it as an informal canvas-embroidery class and leave you to use your imagination to experiment and to create. And, above all, I hope you enjoy yourself.

1 Materials

An obvious starting point for learning about a new craft is the materials. Once you are familiar with the basic materials, you will be ready to learn the techniques. There are only a few items required for canvas embroidery and they are easily obtainable: canvas, wool, needle, scissors, masking tape, and an indelible, felt-tipped pen. Other items, such as drawing paper, tracing paper, glue, blocking board and map pins (push pins), acrylic paints and brush or coloured felt-tipped markers will be needed later, when you begin working on your own designs and transferring them to the canvas. But, in the beginning, when you are just experimenting with the stitches and probably making a sampler, you need not be concerned about anything but the essentials.

Canvas

Canvas is made of either cotton or linen threads woven together leaving square holes in between the vertical (warp) and horizontal (woof) threads. It is these threads and their intersections, called meshes, that are covered when you stitch. The size of canvas is determined by the number of threads or meshes per inch. Thus, number 12 canvas has 12 threads or meshes (either term may be used) to each inch. The more threads a length of canvas has per inch, the finer the weave, and the more stitches will be required to cover it. Canvas ranges in size from 5 meshes to the inch, called rug canvas, to 32 meshes to the inch, which is the finest and is used for petit point. The width varies from 18 inches to 54 inches, with 27 and 36 being the most common. The most popular range of canvas is from 5 to 24 meshes to the inch.

There are two types of canvas: single (a single thread interwoven horizontally and vertically) and double or penelope (two threads interwoven

Photo 1.1 This piece of embroidery shows just some of the variations that can be achieved when using rug canvas as a basis. It is worked with numerous types of wool and cotton and also incorporates raffia. Designed and stitched by Miss N. Dowling.

Photo 1.2 This chair seat, worked between 1740 and 1750, illustrates the effect of separating the threads of penelope canvas. (Crown copyright, Victoria & Albert Museum, London)

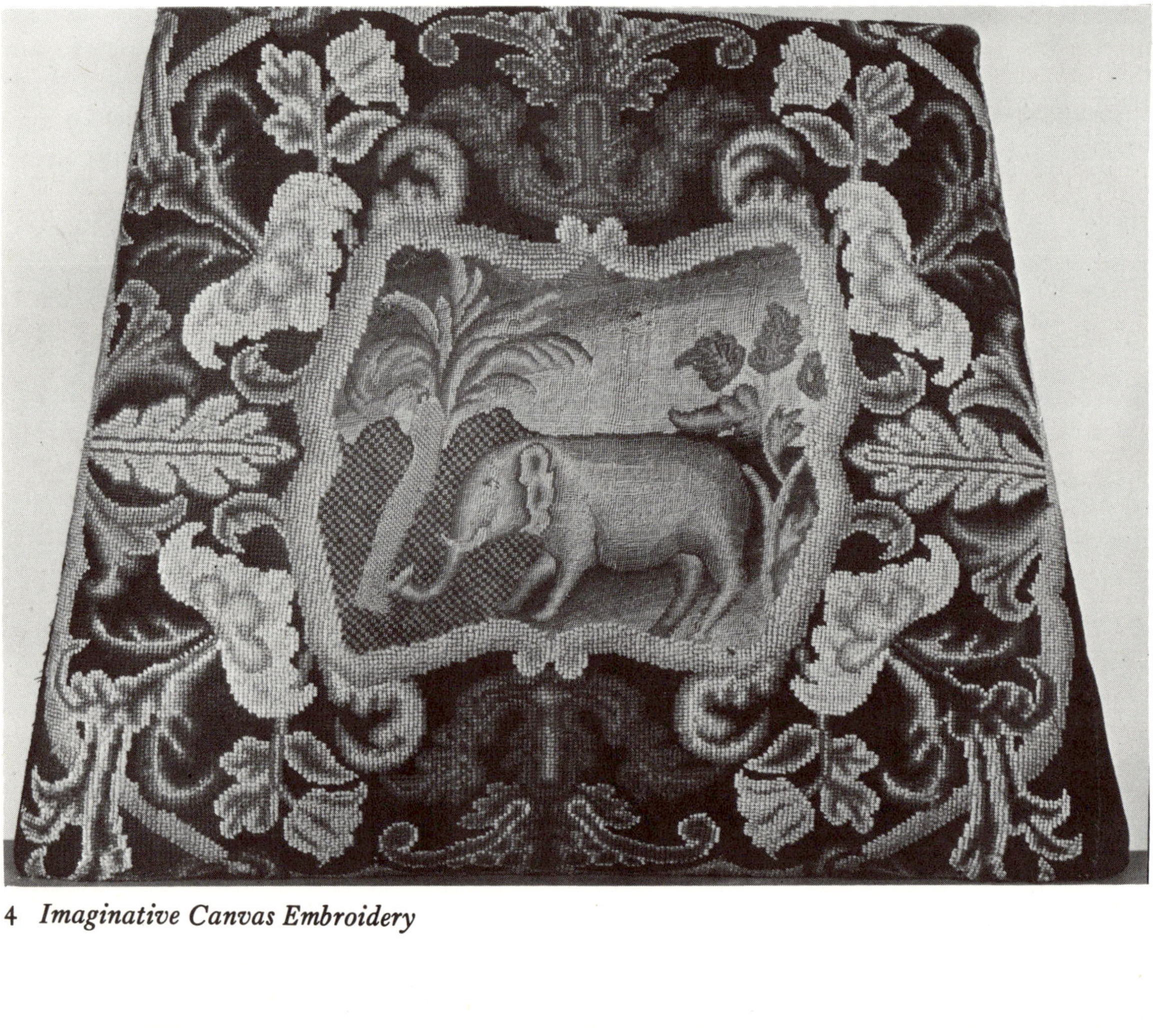

horizontally and vertically). When working on single canvas, it is easier to count the stitches; however, some stitches slip and need more than one thread for support, and are not as full as when worked on penelope canvas. (The stitches that fall into this category are mentioned in Chapter 2.) On penelope canvas, you usually stitch over both threads as if they were one. Most stitches worked on this canvas give better wool coverage because the two threads tend to prevent you pulling the wool too tight; vertical stitches only are an exception. Although it is more difficult to count stitches on penelope canvas, it does have the advantage that you can separate the two threads and work one stitch over each thread; this makes it excellent for detailed work. However, the two threads do make the holes smaller and, on finer sizes, it is often a little troublesome inserting the needle.

When selecting canvas for your project, you must consider the detail in your design. Coarse canvas (with larger holes and fewer meshes to the inch) affords less opportunity for detail in your design, but takes less time to stitch. The size of your project also plays a role in the size of the canvas. Smaller pieces, especially those with intricate designs, are much more effective on fine canvas than coarse. Therefore, consider both factors of detail and size before purchasing your canvas. The most commonly available canvas in Britain is either 12 meshes to the inch single or 10 to the inch double; wool sold in most shops covers this canvas very well. In the United States the wool differs, and there the most commonly used canvas is 10 to the inch single.

Photo 1.3 This panel, framed with velvet, incorporates various types of threads. It was designed and worked by Heather Clark. (Courtesy of Mr J. Parsons)

Needles

The needles used in canvas embroidery are blunt-ended and have long, wide eyes. They are called tapestry needles and range in size from 13 (the larger needles) to 26 (the finer needles). In the United States, the needles range from 13 to 24. The lower-numbered needles are used on the coarser canvas and the higher-numbered needles on the finer canvas. Needles are usually sold in packages of various sizes; the most commonly used needle with both 10 and 12 to the inch canvas is either 17 or 19.

Wool

The type of wool used in canvas embroidery varies according to the number of threads per inch. The two kinds most commonly sold in Great Britain for this craft are crewel wool and tapestry wool. Whichever variety you use, it should be mothproof and colourfast; most wool sold today is both. Usually sold in skeins of one-sixth of an ounce and or one ounce, crewel wool is single stranded, non-divisible, and has a softer texture than tapestry wool. Used singly, one strand of crewel wool covers only very fine canvas. However, the most common practice is to work with a number of strands in the same needle. Thus, you can readily co-ordinate the thickness of crewel wool to your canvas size or your stitch by varying the number of strands you combine to make one length of wool. As a guide, six strands of crewel wool covers 18 to the inch canvas when working the tent stitch. The stitches that require more than the usual thickness of wool are noted in the instructions in Chapter 2. Tapestry wool is a tightly twisted wool available in skeins or by the ounce. It also is non-divisible; to make it thicker, you must combine it with a strand or two of crewel wool, or use it doubled. In Britain, the companies that make crewel wool usually market tapestry wool as well in identical shades. Be certain that you buy the extra strands in the same colours and dye-lots as the tapestry wool or there may well be a slight shade difference. Tapestry wool covers 10 to the inch double, or 12 and 14 to the inch single canvas. In the United States, another kind of wool is available—Persian wool, which consists of three separate strands of wool twisted together. It also is sold in skeins and ounces, and sometimes singly. The full three strands will cover 10 to the inch single canvas; two strands cover 12 and 14 to the inch.

Although canvas embroidery is traditionally stitched with wool, there are many other kinds of threads and cords that can be adapted to use on canvas. You are obviously limited by what is available, but embroidery cottons and silks might be a start. Silk and metallic threads, gold threads, string and macramé cording may also be used; either as overstitching on the wool in the case of the finer threads or directly on the canvas if they will cover the canvas fully. This is one of many areas where experimentation can produce very interesting and original effects.

Before purchasing your wool, you will have to know the wool count for your canvas. Wool count is the amount of each colour of wool you require for your canvas, and the amount varies with the stitch you are working and the size of the canvas you are using. There is no easy method of calculating this. You will have to begin with a sample of the canvas and wool you plan to use for your project. Cover a 1-inch square patch of canvas in the stitch you plan to use, and if you intend to use more than one stitch, work a square-inch patch for each stitch. Note the length of the strand of wool used, and how much is left over or how much more wool you needed. Measure the length and width of each colour area in your design and find the total number of square inches of each colour. Separate the areas by stitching, too, if you are using more than one stitch. It is impossible to be totally accurate with each tiny section of colour, but be as accurate as possible. If in doubt, overestimate rather than underestimate; nothing is worse than running out of wool and going to purchase more, only to discover that there is no more of the dye-lot you need.

Multiply the number of inches of wool used to stitch the patch by the number of square inches in each colour area. Add the total number of square inches of each colour area together and subtract this from the total number of square inches in the entire canvas (the length of the canvas multiplied by the width). This yields the number of inches in the background. Convert the

Photo 1.4 A Tear for Mankind *by Joanne Graham—a panel with hanging 'strings' in a wide, dark frame.*

Photo 1.5 This motif, using crewel wool, soft embroidery cotton and stranded cotton, also incorporates cocktail sticks to raise the wings. Metal purl has been used for the eye of the bird and for highlights on the breast. Designed and stitched by Moyra McNeill.

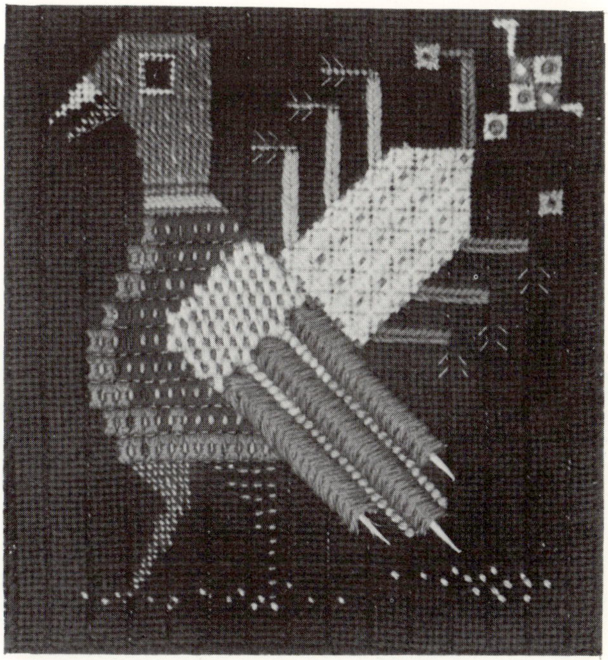

background figure into wool inches, and then convert all the wool inches into wool yards by dividing by 36. Each ounce of tapestry wool is approximately 80 yards long; an ounce of crewel wool is approximately 240 yards long.

As an example, a canvas that measures 10 × 12 inches has a total area of 120 square inches. It has five different colour areas of 24 square inches, 15 square inches, 6 square inches, 16 square inches, and 20 square inches. The total of these colour areas is 81 square inches. The total area of the canvas (120 square inches) minus the total colour area (81 square inches) means that there are 39 square inches of background. If it takes 3 yards to work 1 square inch of the stitch on the appropriate canvas, then the background requires 117 yards of wool (39 multiplied by 3), and the other colour areas require 24 × 3 or 72 yards, 15 × 3 or 45 yards, 6 × 3 or 18 yards, 16 × 3 or 48 yards and 20 × 3 or 60 yards. If you do not want to add up your own wool requirements, the people in your local needlework shop will probably be able to estimate your needs.

Photo 1.6 This panel was designed and worked by Bernard Berthon. (Photographed by M. E. Porter)

Scissors

It is important to have a pair of small scissors handy to clip the ends of the wool on the back of the canvas and to cut any stitches that are not worked properly. A small pair of embroidery scissors is very useful for removing mistakes because the thin blades can easily slip between the wool and the canvas.

To remove an incorrect stitch, clip the stitch on both the front and the back of the canvas. With the needle, carefully pull out a few stitches on both sides of the incorrect stitch, until there is enough wool to weave back into the previous stitches. This, of course, secures each end so that it will not force any other stitches loose. Restitch the section of bare canvas.

Frames

A frame is sometimes mentioned as a requirement for canvas embroidery, but it is actually by no means a necessity. Most assuredly, frames are helpful in preventing distortion and in making stitching easier. On the other hand, putting your work in a frame makes it less portable. Almost exclusively, frames are used with large pieces that are unwieldy because of their size. Only for the most extraordinary projects does one need to go to the expense of a frame.

2 Stitches

Many people who have started learning canvas embroidery, either by buying a kit or a painted canvas, think that there is only one stitch. In fact, there are dozens and dozens of canvas-embroidery stitches; many of them are borrowed from embroidery. What distinguishes one canvas-embroidery stitch from another is the pattern it creates when completed, the method and ease with which it can be worked, its use in a design, the amount of wool it requires and its durability. Some stitches are adaptable for use anywhere, particularly in odd shapes or the background, while others that require a specific number of rows for completion are less suitable for general application. By blending all types of stitches in one canvas, rather than using one single stitch, you will attain the full richness of canvas embroidery.

To simplify what is so often presented as a barrage of unrelated stitches, think of canvas embroidery as being of three basic types: diagonal, horizontal or vertical. A number of stitches such as the tent stitch (a simple diagonal stitch) involve an easy two-step method of drawing the wool to the front of the canvas and returning it to the back. Others are combinations that are worked in three or more steps, as in the case of the Smyrna-cross stitch (a diagonal, vertical and horizontal stitch) or the double leviathan stitch (a diagonal, vertical and horizontal stitch). Some stitches are worked over one mesh, others over two or more. In fact, a few stitches can be worked over two, three, or four meshes, depending upon your design.

The most sensible method of teaching yourself canvas-embroidery stitches is to practice simultaneously all the stitches that are worked in a similar manner. The fifty stitches presented in this book have been classified into seven categories, but you will not find these classifications elsewhere. In using them, I hope to create a logical order for your learning pattern, rather than to overwhelm you with different stitches, sometimes similar in name, but often worked in a dissimilar manner. The seven categories are as follows: diagonal, crossed diagonal, patterned diagonal, patterned vertical, horizontal, combination, and looped. The relevance of the classification titles will become clearer when you begin to work with the stitches.

Before discussing the stitches in detail, there are a few preliminaries with which you should become familiar. There is, for example, a 'right' way to thread a tapestry needle and a specific way to begin and end your stitches. By adopting these routines, you will avoid the disappointment of uneven stitches which could ruin the effect of your entire piece.

Preparing the wool

First you must cut the wool to workable lengths. Wool frays when it is continually pulled through canvas and eventually produces some stitches which are thinner than others. Cut the wool into approximately 15-inch lengths if

Photo 2.1 The materials for this evening bag, worked on fine single-mesh canvas, include metal threads which give interesting highlights to the piece. (Courtesy of The Embroiderers' Guide; donated by Miss Hornblower)

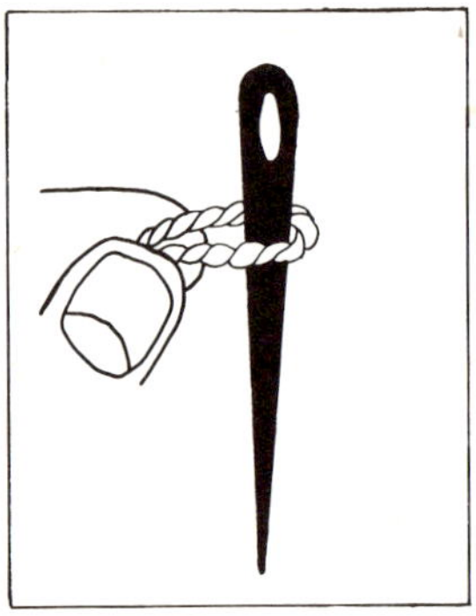

Fig. 2.1 Threading the needle: stage one.

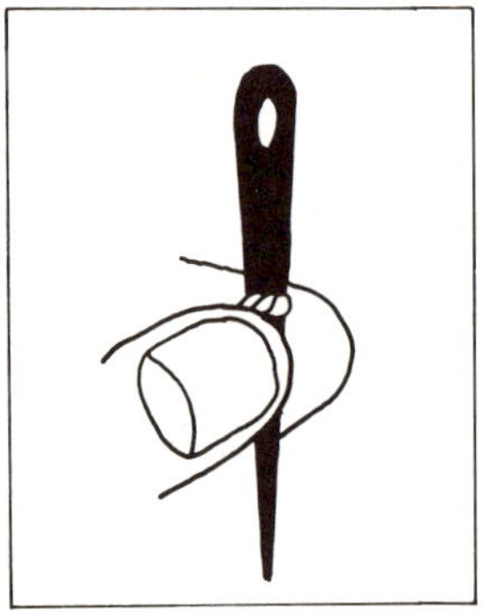

Fig. 2.2 Threading the needle: stage two.

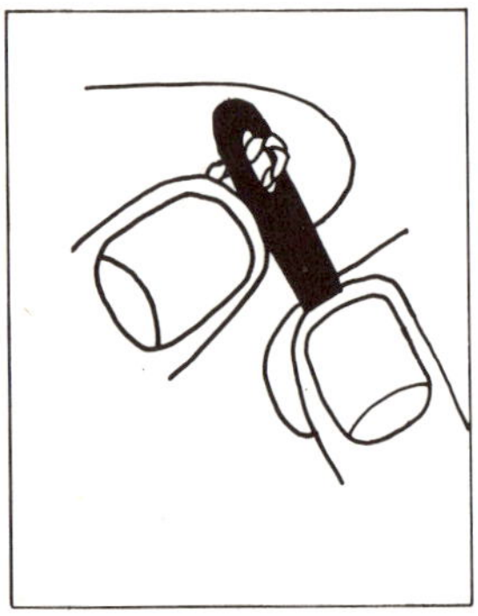

Fig. 2.3 Threading the needle: stage three.

you are stitching petit point canvas (28 to 20 meshes to the inch) and 24- to 26-inch lengths for medium (18 to 10 meshes to the inch) and larger sized canvas. If you see the wool becoming fuzzy while you are stitching, it is wise to finish off that strand of wool, and avoid marring the smooth texture of your canvas with a few stitches of obviously varying thicknesses.

Threading the Needle

Next thread the needle. Rather than inserting the yarn into the eye of the needle–the technique with an ordinary sewing needle—the eye of the tapestry needle is placed over the wool.

1. Taking the needle in your right hand and the wool in your left hand, loop the wool around the needle, catching the ends of the wool with your thumb and forefinger (see Fig. 2.1).
2. Slide your fingers up the wool until the loop is tight around the needle (see Fig. 2.2).
3. Squeezing the wool tightly between your fingers, carefully slip the needle out of the loop.
4. Still holding the wool between your thumb and forefinger, place the eye of the needle over the tiny loop of wool, manoeuvring the needle until you can pull the wool all the way through the eye (see Fig. 2.3).

Securing ends

Stitching the entire surface of the canvas makes it imperative that each strand of wool is secured both at the beginning and the end. If this is not done properly, individual stitches may pull free and loosen other stitches. To begin a new strand of wool, draw the needle and the wool to the front of the canvas, leaving about an inch to an inch and a half free on the back of the canvas. Press this end of wool flush against the back of the canvas in the direction in which the next stitches will be made and hold the wool in place with your finger. Cover this end with the next few stitches. To finish off the strand, weave the remaining few inches back through the last stitches. After removing the needle, clip the ends closely so that they do not get caught in any subsequent strands or pulled to the front of the canvas, leaving a short fluffy bit of wool on the front which is difficult to return to the back.

Tension

Tension is also important. To maintain a smooth texture and to be certain of covering the canvas adequately, take special care to keep your stitches even, and do not pull the wool too tight. Pulling the wool very taut flattens your stitches and causes bare canvas to show, increases the natural distortion of the canvas and contributes to wool fraying.

You may find that your wool becomes twisted as you stitch; this is a natural result of the action of stitching, but twisted wool produces uneven

Photo 2.2 On the left is a pillow worked in tent stitch, on the right is the tramé canvas of the same design. Both the tramé canvas and the wool are available from Luxury Needlepoint Tapestries, 36 Beauchamp Place, London SW3.

thicknesses in your stitches and alters the texture of your piece. When the wool does become twisted, simply hold the canvas upside down, so that the needle and yarn hang free, and let the wool untwist itself.

Tramé

A few canvas-embroidery stitches are worked over tramé. Tramé is an understitching of long basting-type stitches worked in vertical rows over the horizontal threads of the canvas; the canvas-embroidery stitch is then worked over the tramé. The purpose of tramé is twofold: it may be used to add body to a stitch and it may be used to outline a design or to indicate the placement of colours. (Most European canvases are made this way.) Tramé can be laid on either type of canvas, but must be in irregular rows or ridges will form. Lay all the tramé first, then work the canvas-embroidery stitch.

1. To tramé penelope canvas, the wool is always stitched between the two horizontal threads so that it covers the mesh. Draw the unknotted wool to the front of the canvas at A, between the two horizontal threads, slightly in front of the mesh at which you intend to begin stitching; see Fig. 2.4. Leave a 2-inch end loose at the back of the canvas and catch it in the canvas-embroidery stitch later. Make a stitch any length—five meshes, for example—and return to the back at B, again between the two horizontal threads. Come to the front at C, between the two horizontal threads, one row below stitch AB. Return to the back at D, in this instance three meshes wide. Continue working down your canvas until you have completed the section. Turn the can-

vas and work the second row of different sized stitches. Continue working in this manner, taking care to vary the sizes of the stitches and to turn the canvas at the end of each row.

2. To tramé single canvas, the wool is laid across the threads of the canvas. On this type canvas, tramé is most effectively used to add body to stitches worked over two vertical threads; therefore, the tramé is laid over every other row of threads. Leaving a 2-inch end free at the back of the canvas, begin at A, as indicated in Fig. 2.5. Make the stitch any length and return to the back at B, then come to the front at C, two rows below. Make the second stitch at D, a different length than the first. Continue as advised above, turning the canvas at the end of the row and varying the lengths of the stitches.

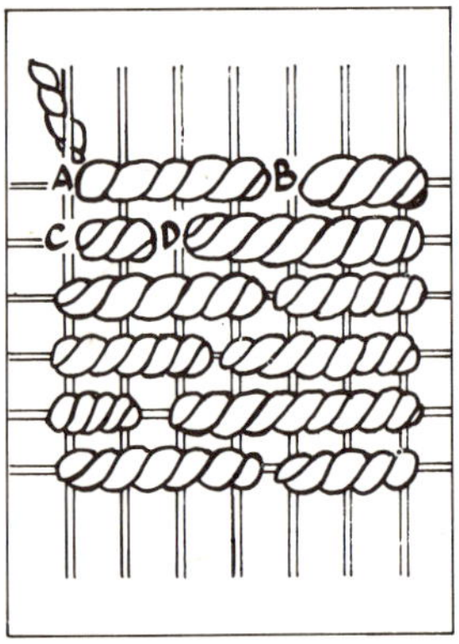

Fig. 2.4 Tramé stitching on penelope canvas.

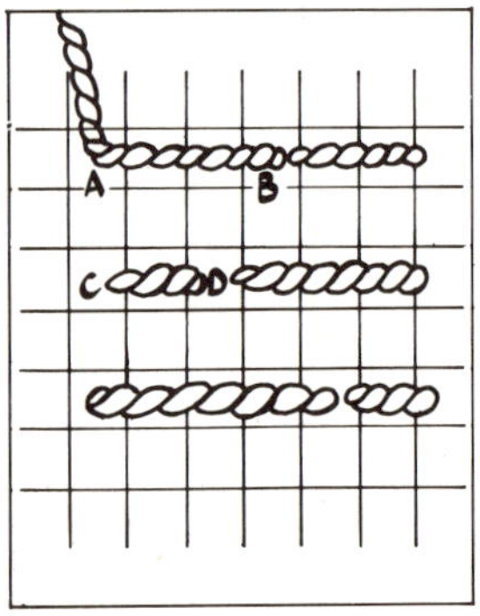

Fig. 2.5 Tramé stitching on single canvas.

To figure the amount of wool needed to tramé one square inch of canvas, divide the number of meshes per inch of the canvas by two, and add 2 inches. For example, if the project is to be stitched on 12 to the inch canvas and the design requires 15 square inches of tramé, you will need $3\frac{1}{3}$ yards of extra wool, i.e. 12 divided by 2 equals 6; 6 plus 2 equals 8 inches of wool per each square inch of tramé; 8 × 15 equals 120 inches or $3\frac{1}{3}$ yards. Remember to calculate each different coloured area of tramé separately.

In discussing various ideas and techniques with your friends, you will find that some stitches have more than one name. For example, the tent stitch in Britain is called the continental stitch in America. (For that matter, the craft itself has three colloquial names—tapestry, needlepoint or canvas embroidery, depending upon where you are.) The alternate names of stitches are mentioned here, so that you will be familiar with them and will know which stitch your friends are talking about, whatever name they use.

You will also discover that there can be more than one valid way to work a stitch. Each method has its advantages; some provide a thicker backing, while others use more wool. As long as the stitch looks as it should and the same technique is used over the entire canvas, the results should be satisfactory. Purists may not agree with this, but so much of what is new in crafts comes from experimentation that I think it is foolhardy to discourage it.

One final word: regardless of the method, remember to be consistent and precise when you stitch. One or two stitches worked differently immediately attract attention and can ruin the effect of the piece. There is little sense in spending hours working a canvas if it is stitched haphazardly; the results are never as satisfying.

Note: Left-handed embroiderers will note that the drawings and instructions are written with the right-handed person in mind. To translate the drawings, turn the book upside down and follow the instructions. Or, if reading upside down is impossible, trace the drawing on to the layout or tracing paper and turn the paper to the wrong side, label the drawing and follow the directions.

Diagonal Stitches

The diagonal stitches are the most frequently used and most commonly known canvas-embroidery stitches. They are simple diagonal stitches slanting from left to right, covering one or more meshes. As a group, they tend to distort the canvas more than the vertical or horizontal stitches, but this blocks out of the finished canvas. The use of each individual stitch varies, but diagonal stitches are adaptable to almost any design requirements.

Tent or Continental Stitch

One of the most popular canvas-embroidery stitches, the tent stitch is also used in petit point. It is a plain diagonal stitch that is quite easy to work and, because of its flexibility, it is excellent for backgrounds and filling shapes (see photo 2.3). Pieces stitched in the tent stitch can withstand a substantial amount of wear for it provides a good backing. Although this stitch pulls the canvas out of shape, the distortion will be rectified when blocking the finished canvas. Since tent stitch is *always* worked from right to left, you must turn the canvas upside down to work the even-numbered rows and again right side up to work the odd-numbered rows. The stitch can be worked on both single and penelope canvas.

1. Draw the wool to the front of the canvas at A and insert the needle at B, diagonally to the right and one row above A as shown in Fig. 2.6. Pull the wool to the back of the canvas.
2. Return the needle to the front of the canvas at C, beside A. Pull the wool to the front again.
3. Insert the needle into D, diagonally to the right of C and next to B. Pull the wool to the back and continue in this manner to the end of the row.
4. To stitch the second row, turn the canvas upside down and bring the

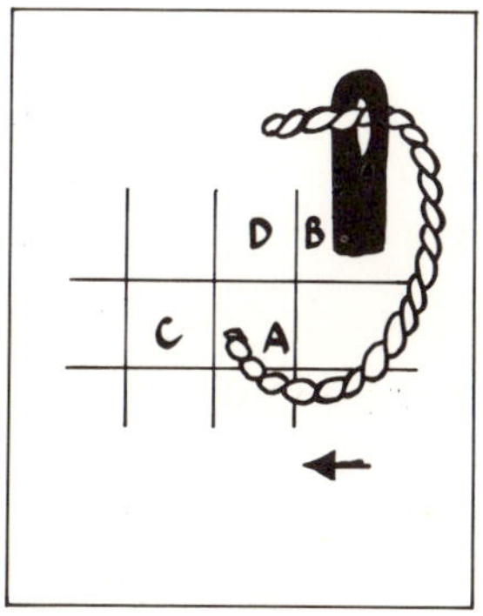

Fig. 2.6 Tent stitch: the start of the first row.

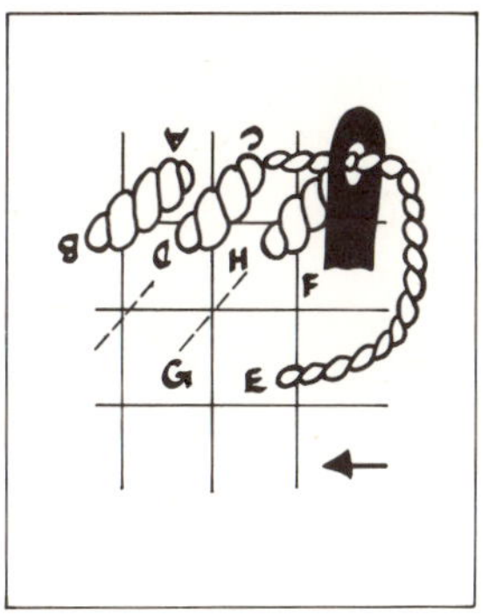

Fig. 2.7 Tent stitch: the start of the second row. Note that the canvas has been turned.

Photo 2.3 Tent or continental stitch.

needle to the front at E (see Fig. 2.7). Insert the needle at F, diagonally to the right and one row above E. Continue as before—coming to the front at G, and returning to the back at H (which will be shared with the last stitch in the first row).

5. To work the third row, turn the canvas the right way around and stitch as previously.

Half-cross Stitch

The half-cross stitch is another way of working the basic diagonal stitch (see photo 2.4). Its flexibility makes it useful for backgrounds and filling spaces. This stitch is best worked on penelope canvas because it needs the two threads to support it; it is less effectively stitched on single canvas. The half-cross is worked completely opposite to the tent (continental) stitch in that it is always worked from left to right, and again you must turn the canvas upside down at the beginning of each row. Although the half-cross does not provide as firm a backing as the tent (continental) stitch, it is more economical with wool. This stitch pulls the canvas out of shape, but this is easily rectified when you block the finished piece.

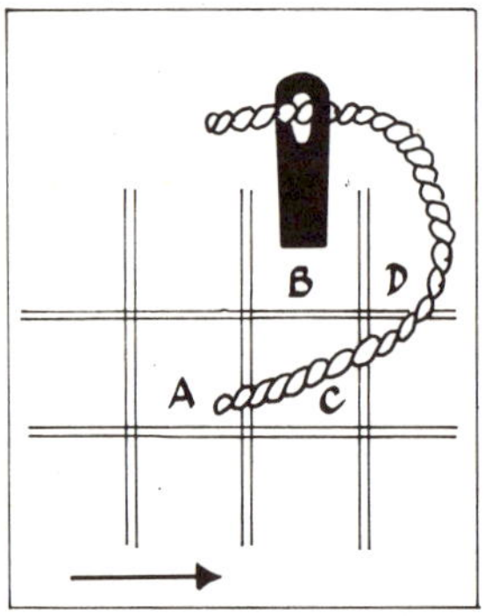

Fig. 2.8 Half-cross stitch: the start of the first row.

1. Bring the needle to the front of the canvas at A. Insert the needle at B, diagonally to the right and one thread above A. See Fig. 2.8.

2. Return the needle to the front at C, directly below B. Insert the needle at D, diagonally to the right of C and beside B. Continue in this manner to the end of the row. (See Fig. 2.9).

3. To work the second row, turn the canvas upside down and bring the needle to the front at E, one thread below the first row. Insert the needle at F, diagonally to the right and one thread above E. F will be shared with the last stitch in the first row. See Fig. 2.9. Continue to the end of the row.

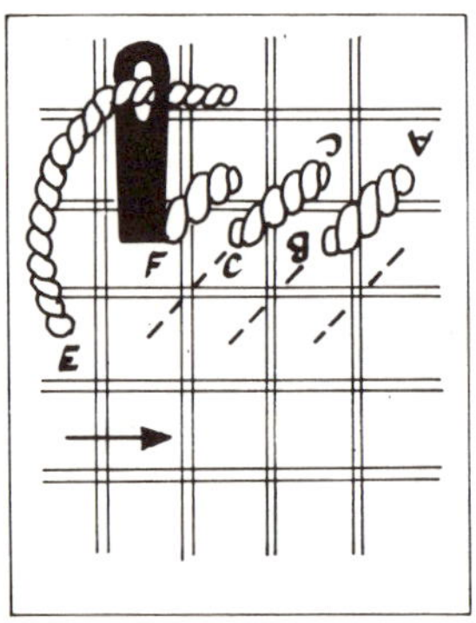

Fig. 2.9 Half-cross stitch: the start of the second row. The canvas has been turned.

Photo 2.4 Half-cross stitch.

4. Turn the canvas to work the third row, and again for each subsequent row.

Note: A combination of the tent (continental) stitch and the half-cross stitch worked on large penelope canvas is called 'quick-point'. The first row is worked from right to left in the tent stitch and the second row from left to right in the half-cross stitch, thus avoiding the necessity of turning the canvas at the end of each row.

Basket-weave or Diagonal Tent Stitch

Named for the pattern it makes on the back of the canvas, the basket-weave stitch is a variant of a basic diagonal stitch (see photo 2.5). The criss-cross, closely woven backing makes durability one of its advantages. Because it must be worked in diagonal rows, the basket-weave is not very adaptable to small, irregular shapes, but it is excellent for background work and can be used to fill shapes which have been outlined in the tent stitch. There is no canvas distortion when this stitch is used in a piece, and it may be worked on both penelope and single canvas. Of the three methods of stitching a basic diagonal stitch, this is by far the most interesting and fun to do; indeed, it is the only one that has a stitching rhythm.

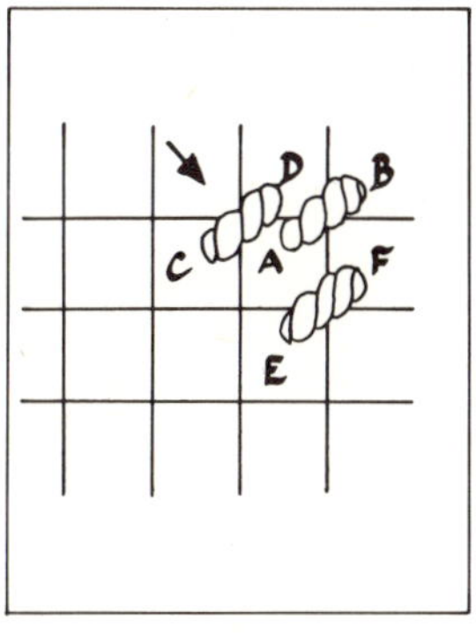

Fig. 2.10 The first two rows of basket-weave.

1. This stitch must always be started by the right-handed stitcher in the top right-hand corner of the design; left-handed people start in the lower left-hand corner. Begin by drawing the wool through A and returning to the back of the canvas at B, forming the first row of one stitch. See Fig. 2.10.
2. The second row consists of two diagonal stitches, CD and EF, worked on the diagonal of the canvas, as shown in Fig. 2.10.

Photo 2.5 Basket-weave stitch.

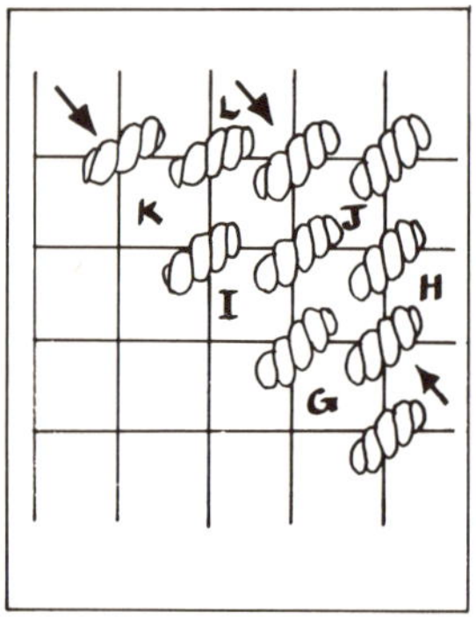

Fig. 2.11 The progression of basket-weave stitching.

3. The third row is worked on the diagonal from the bottom of the design to the top, consisting of stitches GH, IJ, and KL.

4. The fourth row is worked on the diagonal in the opposite direction, i.e., from the top towards the bottom of the design, the fifth row back again from the bottom to the top diagonal, and so forth. See Fig. 2.11.

Note: You must alternate your rows properly or a ridge will form between any two rows that are worked in the same direction. Do not skip to another part of the design when working this stitch because the rows may not alternate when they meet. To help remember in which direction you are working, stop stitching in the middle of a row rather than at the end.

Slanting Gobelin Stitch

An elongated tent stitch, the slating Gobelin is one of four Gobelin stitches—two of these are simple diagonal stitches, the third is a crossed diagonal stitch and the last a vertical stitch. This diagonal stitch covers two, three, four or five threads (see photo 2.6). As the number of threads increases, the stitch loses some of its hardwearing and snagproof quality, and you may well have to double your wool or add an extra strand to be certain that the canvas is covered adequately. The slanting Gobelin may be worked on both single and penelope canvas, and in either direction without having to turn the canvas. It is most popularly used as a background stitch, especially as it is quick to work.

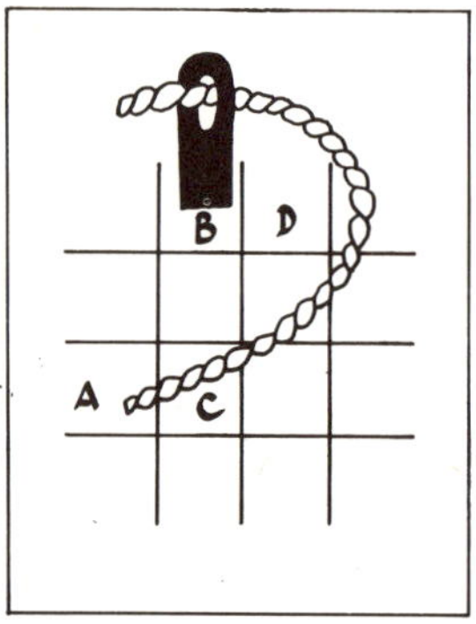

Fig. 2.12 Slanting Gobelin stitch: the start of the first row.

1. Bring the needle to the front of the canvas at A and insert the needle at B, diagonally to the right and two (three, four or five) meshes above A. See Fig. 2.12.

2. Return the needle to the front of the canvas at C, alongside A and insert the needle at D, one thread diagonally to the right of C, and alongside B. Continue in the same manner to the end of the row.

3. To work the second row, bring the needle to the front of the canvas at E, two (three, four or five) threads below and one thread to the left of the last stitch in the first row. See Fig. 2.13. Insert the needle into F, one thread to the right and two (three, four or five) threads above E; F will be shared with the last stitch in the first row. Continue to the end of the row.

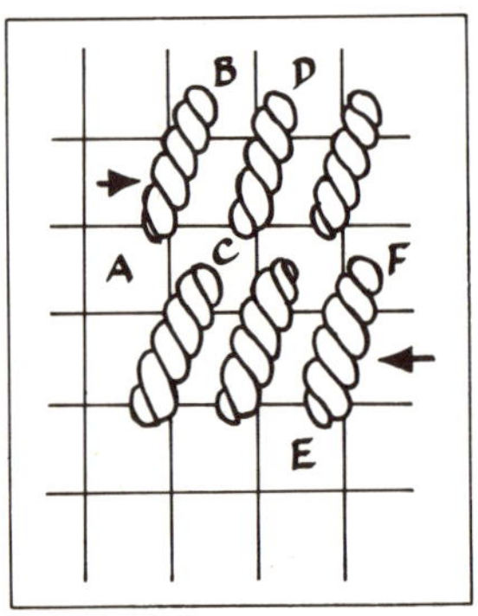

Fig. 2.13 Slanting Gobelin stitch: the first two rows.

Note: Remember that the slanting Gobelin requires at least two horizontal threads per stitch to complete; the length of the stitch should be taken into account when you are planning your design (i.e., be sure to have an even number of rows if the stitch is two threads in height or a number of rows which is evenly divisible by three, four or five if the stitch is longer).

Rep or Aubusson Stitch.

The rep stitch consists of two small diagonal stitches, each worked over two vertical and one of the two horizontal threads of penelope canvas (see photo

2.7). It is slow to work and distorts the canvas, but because it is half the size of the tent (continental) stitch, it blends very well with the latter and is excellent for detailed work. There are a number of different ways to work the rep stitch; I have chosen the one that I feel is least awkward and uses the wool most economically. With this method the stitch is worked in vertical rows.

Note: The threads of the penelope canvas are enlarged in these drawings, to make it easier to understand the stitch.

Photo 2.6 Slanting Gobelin stitch.

Photo 2.7 Rep or aubusson stitch.

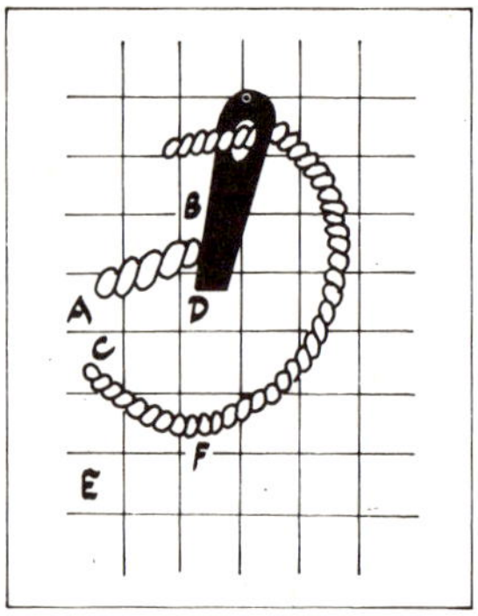

Fig. 2.14 Rep or aubusson stitch: the start of the first row.

1. Bring the needle to the front at A, as shown in Fig. 2.14, between the two horizontal threads. Insert the needle at B, two vertical threads to the right and diagonally above. Return to the front at C, one thread below A, and insert it at D, between the two horizontal threads.

2. To work the third stitch, come up at E, between the two horizontal threads and insert the needle at F, two vertical threads to the right and diagonally above. Continue in this way to the end of the row.

3. To stitch the second row, turn the canvas and continue as before coming to the front at G in Fig. 2.15 and inserting the needle at H, coming up at I and going back to J, coming up at K and returning at L.

4. Turn the canvas at the end of each row.

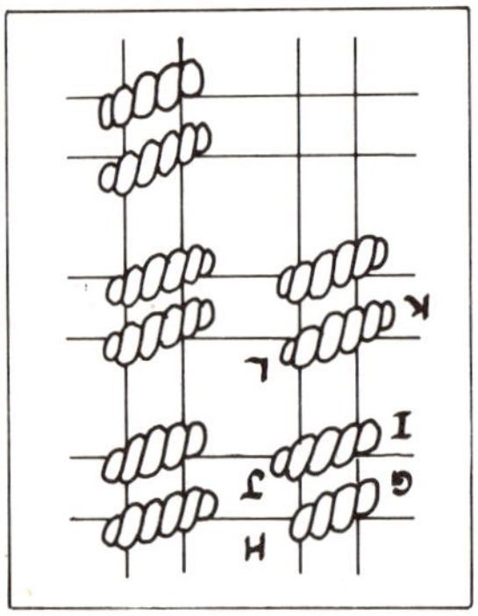

Fig. 2.15 Rep or aubusson stitch: the start of the second row. Note that the canvas has been turned.

Interlocking or Encroaching Gobelin Stitch

This relative of the slanting Gobelin stitch may be worked over any number from two to five threads of the canvas (see photo 2.8). The interlocking Gobelin provides a hardwearing surface on both front and back of the canvas. Like the slanting Gobelin, as the length of the interlocking Gobelin stitch increases, the firmness of the backing and the surface decreases and you may have to adjust your wool to cover the canvas completely. Because this stitch is quick to work, it makes an excellent background stitch, despite its tendency to distort the shape of the canvas. Blocking and stretching the canvas rectifies this. Both single and penelope canvas may be used with this stitch which can be worked in either direction, right to left or left to right, without turning the canvas.

1. Bright the needle to the front of the canvas at A. Insert the needle at B, one thread to the right, and two (three, four or five, depending upon your choice of stitch length) threads above A. See Fig. 2.16. Return the needle to the front at C, beside A and two rows below B. Continue to the end of the row.

2. To stitch the second row, bring the needle to the front of the canvas at D, two threads below the bottom of the last stitch in the first row and return to the back at E, two threads above and one to the right of D. Return to the front of the canvas at F, to the left of D, and insert the needle at G, between the last two stitches in the first row. Continue to the end of the row. Be careful not to split the wool as you stitch.

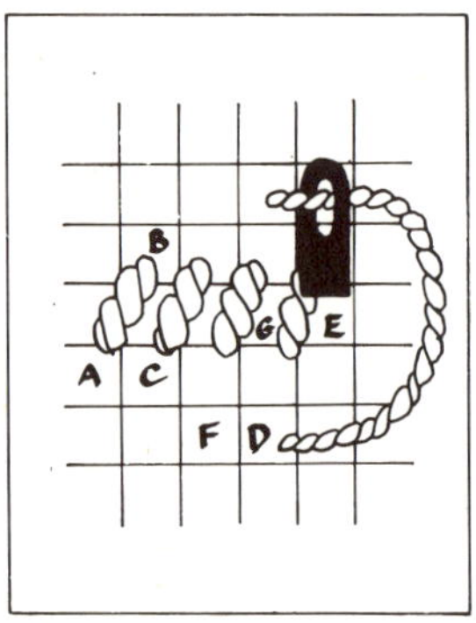

Fig. 2.16 Interlocking Gobelin stitch. Note how the rows overlap.

Note: This is another stitch which requires special consideration when it is included in a design because it must have at least three horizontal threads—two threads for the first row and one more for the second interlocking row—to complete the stitch.

Encroaching Oblique Stitch

The encroaching oblique stitch (photo 2.9) is similar to the interlocking

Photo 2.8 *Encroaching Gobelin stitch.*

Photo 2.9 *Encroaching oblique stitch.*

Gobelin but more slanted. The backing this stitch provides on both sides of the canvas is thick and smooth. Because it uses less wool than interlocking Gobelin, the encroaching oblique may be incorporated into a design if you are trying to conserve wool. It is quick to work and you don't have to turn the canvas because the rows are alternatively worked from left to right and right to left. This is a useful and attractive background stitch which does not distort either single or penelope canvas. As you stitch each row after the first, take extra care to insert the needle in the correct hole; do not split the wool as you stitch.

1. Bring the needle to the front of the canvas at A in Fig. 2.17. Insert the needle at B, four threads to the right and one thread below A.

2. Return to the front at C, two threads to the right of A. Insert the needle at D, two threads to the right of B. Continue in this fashion to the end of the row.

3. To stitch the second row, bring the needle to the front at E (Fig. 2.18) one thread below the last stitch in the first row. Insert the needle at D, four threads to the left and one above E. Stitch ED will share D with stitch CD. Return to the front at F, two threads to the left of E. Insert the needle at B, again four threads to the left and one above F. Continue to the end of the row in this manner, always being certain not to split the wool of the stitches in the previous row.

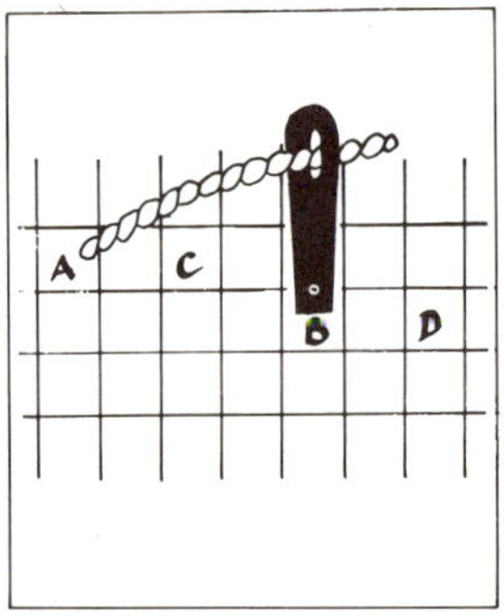

Fig. 2.17 Encroaching Gobelin stitch: positioning the first two stitches.

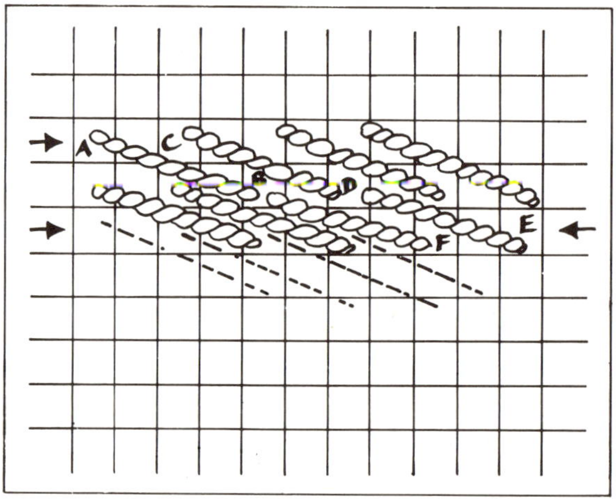

Fig. 2.18 Encroaching Gobelin stitch: the first two rows and positioning for the third.

Photo 2.10 Kalem stitch.

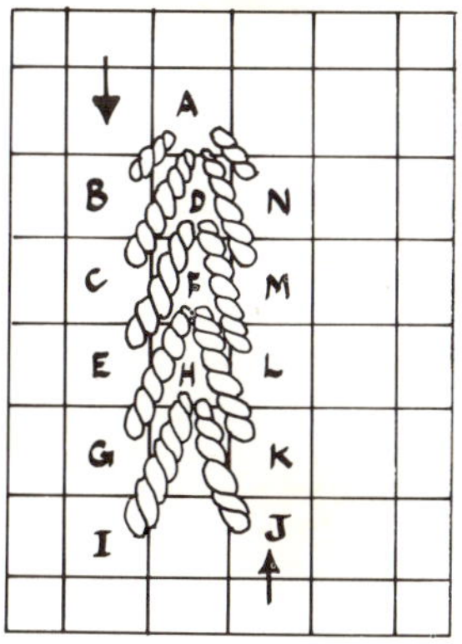

Fig. 2.19 Kalem stitch: the first two rows.

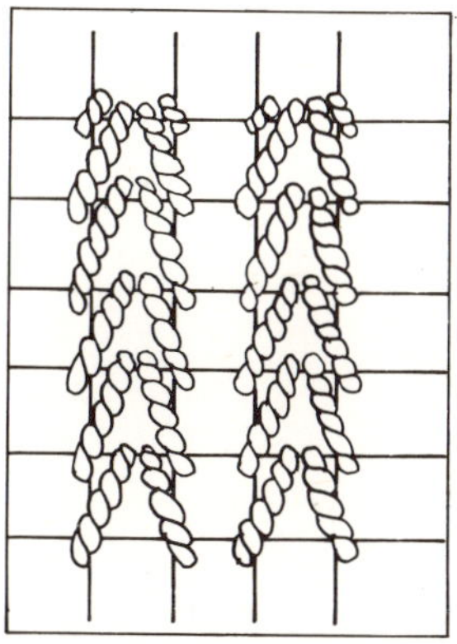

Fig. 2.20 Successive rows of kalem stitching produce a pattern which resembles knitting.

Kalem Stitch or Reverse Tent Stitch

Both the kalem stitch and the knitting stitch (which is described in the following section) make patterns which resemble knitting (photo 2.10). Worked vertically, the kalem combines beautifully with the knitting stitch on the same canvas either as background or for detailed work. However, the kalem is slow to stitch and consumes wool very quickly. It may be worked on both types of canvas.

1. Begin at A as shown in Fig. 2.19 and insert the needle at B, diagonally to the left of A. Return to the front at A and insert the needle at C, one thread below B. Come to the surface at D, one thread to the right of B. Insert the needle at E, come to the front at F; insert the needle at G, come to the front at H; return again to the back at I and continue in this fashion to the end of your row. The stitch may be as long as your needs dictate.
2. To stitch the second row, which is worked from the bottom of the canvas to the top, bring the needle to the front at J and return to the back at H; come to the front at K, one thread above J, and return to the back at F. Come to the front at L, return to the back at D; come to the front at M, return to the back at A; come to the front at N and finish the row by returning to the back at A. Fig. 2.20 shows how the rows of the kalem fit together.

Note: If you find it awkward working this stitch from top to bottom and bottom to top, turn the canvas on its side.

Knitting Stitch

The other member of the pair of stitches that resemble knitting when completed, the knitting stitch (see photo 2.11), is worked horizontally, rather

Photo 2.11 Knitting stitch.

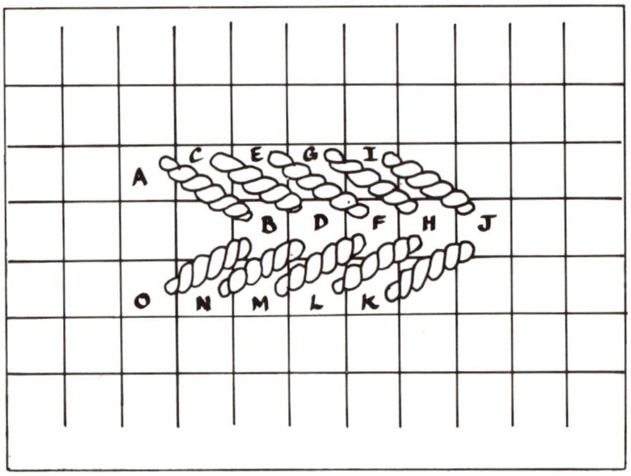

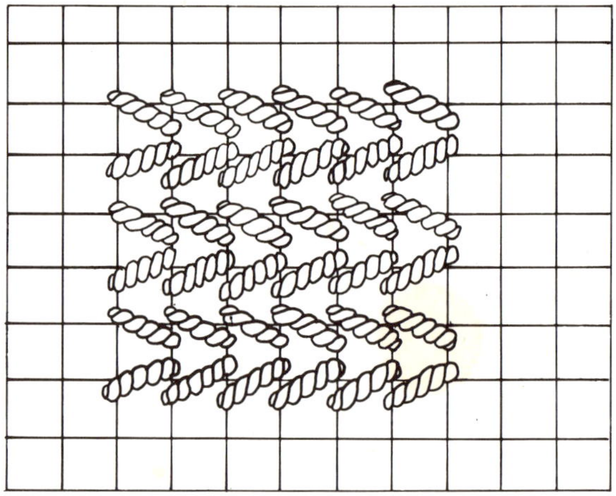

Fig. 2.21 Knitting stitch resembles kalem stitch but is worked horizontally.

Fig. 2.22 Complete rows of knitting stitch make this pattern on the canvas.

than vertically as the kalem stitch. Useful for backgrounds or detailed shapes, the knitting stitch is tedious to work and requires a lot of wool, but it can be stitched on both types of canvas and does not pull the canvas out of shape.

1. Beginning at A as shown in Fig. 2.21, insert the needle at B, one thread below and two to the right of A. Return to the front at C, immediately to the right of A, and insert the needle at D, beside B. Come to the front at E, return to the back at F; come to the front at G and to the back at H; return to the front at I and to the back at J. The length of the row is governed by your needs, as long as there are two horizontal threads over which the stitch can be worked.

2. Fig. 2.21 also shows how to work the second row. Begin by drawing the needle to the front of the canvas at K, two threads to the left, and one below J, and complete by inserting the needle at J, which is shared with stitch IJ. Come to the front at H and return to the back at L. Come to the front at F and return to the back at M. Come to the front at D and insert the needle at N. Return to the front at B, and insert the needle to complete the row at O. Fig. 2.22 shows how subsequent rows fit together on the canvas.

Note: If there is a noticeable gap at the end of the row (between A and O, Fig. 2.21) insert a horizontal fill-in stitch.

Crossed Diagonal Stitches

There are two types of crossed diagonal stitches: those that have crossed diagonal stitches of the same length, such as the cross stitch, and those whose crossing stitches are of different lengths, as with the long-and-short oblique. Some crossed diagonals are completed as individual stitches, while others are worked in two steps by stitching all the diagonals in one direction first and then returning to cross them. The uses of the crossed diagonals are varied—you may even want to work an entire canvas in one of them.

Cross Stitch

One of the many stitches borrowed from embroidery, the cross stitch is also one of the oldest stitches (photo 2.12). Because the same mesh of canvas is covered twice, it is a slow stitch to work, but it provides a sturdy backing. The cross stitch can be worked on both types of canvas, but like the half-cross stitch, makes a neater appearance on penelope canvas. There are two methods of stitching the cross stitch—either by making a row of half-cross stitches from left to right and returning on the same row, crossing the half-crosses from right to left, or by completing each individual stitch before going on to the next one. The first method is quicker to work, but provides less backing; use the second method when stitching single canvas because it produces a neater finish. However, whichever method or type of canvas you are using, you must be sure to cross each stitch in the *same direction.* This is a very adaptable stitch that can be used for backgrounds, filling both large and small spaces, and stitching for emphasis.

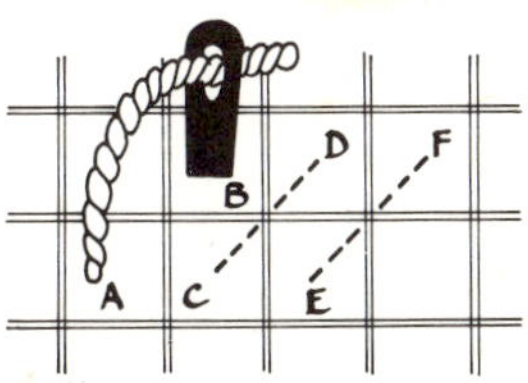

Fig. 2.23 Traditional cross stitch worked in rows: the first row.

The Cross Stitch worked in rows

1. Begin at A in Fig. 2.23 and insert the needle at B, diagonally to the right and one thread above A (as you would when stitching the half-cross stitch. Return to the front at C, one thread below B. Insert the needle at D, level with B, and come to the front at E. Return to the back at F and continue in this manner to the end of the row.

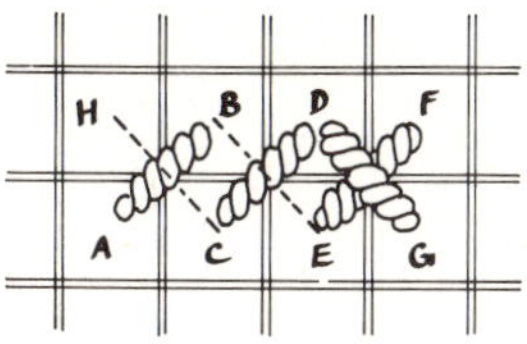

Fig. 2.24 Cross stitch: the second row, to make the crosses.

2. To work the second half of the stitch, come to the front of the canvas at G as shown in Fig. 2.24. Insert the needle at D, diagonally to the left and one thread above G, completing the first cross. Come to the front at E, directly below D. Continue in this manner, inserting the needle at B, returning to the surface at C, inserting the needle at H.

Photo 2.12 Cross stitch.

The Cross Stitch worked as an individual stitch

1. Starting at A as shown in Fig. 2.25, insert the needle at B, diagonally to the right and one thread above A. Come to the front of the canvas at C and complete the stitch by inserting the needle at D, one thread diagonally to the left of C. Finish off on the back of the canvas.

2. If you are working on single canvas and want to stitch a row of cross stitches, bring the needle to the front at C, to begin the second stitch (see Fig. 2.26). Insert the needle at E and return to the front of the canvas at F. Insert the needle at B to complete the second stitch.

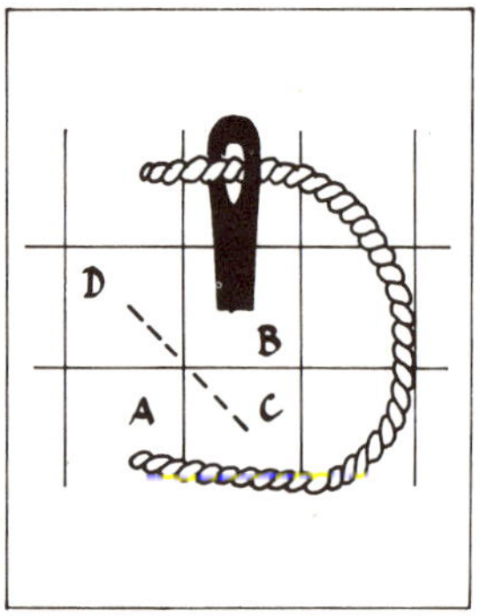

Fig. 2.25 Making an individual cross stitch: the first diagonal.

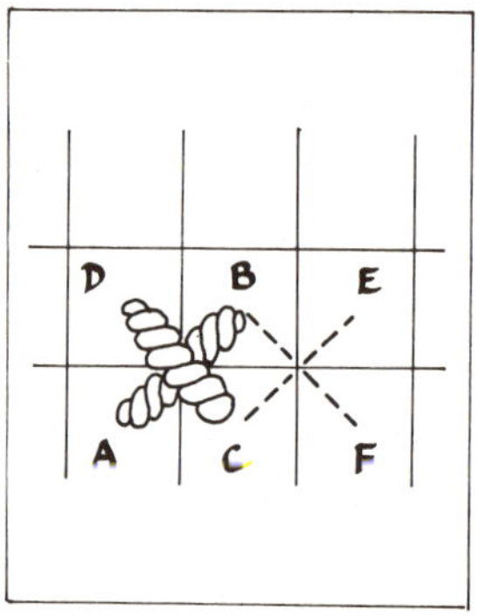

Fig. 2.26 Completing an individual cross stitch. The position for the second stitch is indicated by dotted lines; note that the crosses must be made in the same direction.

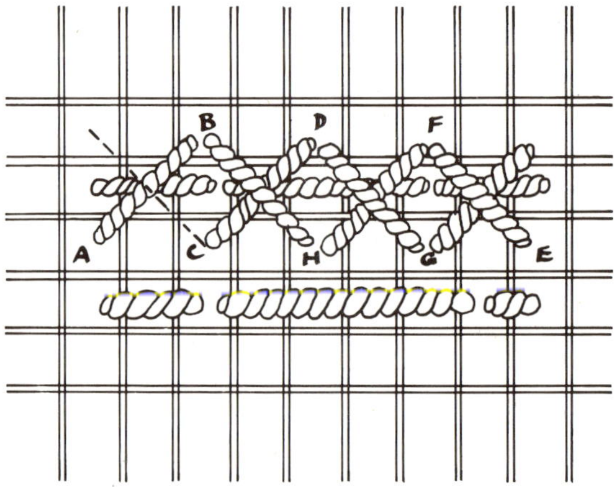

Fig. 2.27 Cross-stitch tramé, a good background filler.

Cross-Stitch Tramé

The cross-stitch tramé (photo 2.13) is worked in rows using the same method as the simple cross stitch but over two vertical and horizontal threads of the canvas. The combination of tramming and the increase in size makes this stitch quite unmistakable from the simple cross stitch, both in appearance and texture; it can be worked on both types of canvas. Remember to do irregular-length stitches when tramming, as already mentioned on page 14. This stitch is good for backgrounds and as a filler.

1. Prepare a section of canvas with tramé every other row.

2. Bring the needle to the front of the canvas at A, return to the back at B, two threads to the right, and two above A (see Fig. 2.27). Return to the front at C, level with A, and return to the back at D, two threads to the right and two above C. Continue to the end of the row.

3. To work the second half of the stitch, come to the front at E and insert the needle at F. Come to the front at G and insert the needle at D. Come to the front again at H and continue in the same fashion to the end of the row.

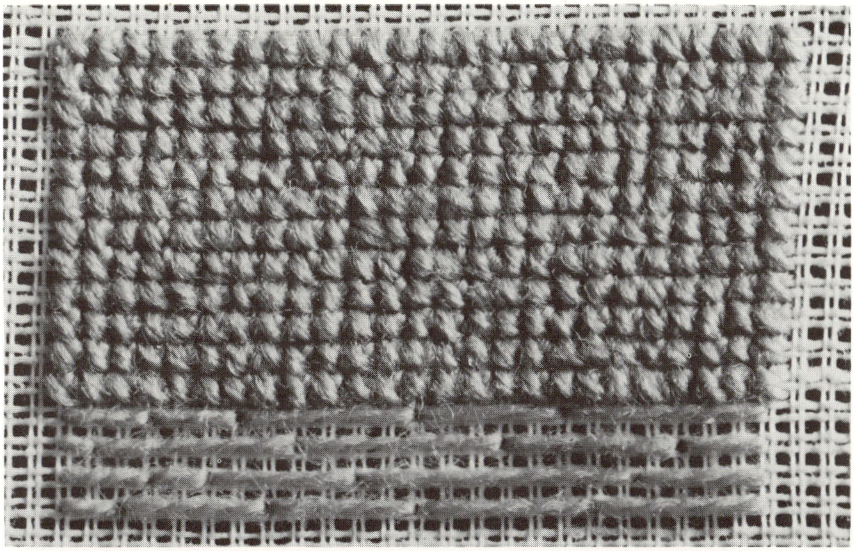

Photo 2.13 Cross-stitch tramé.

Photo 2.14 Oblong cross stitch.

Oblong Cross Stitch

Worked in two steps, the oblong cross stitch is similar to the cross-stitch tramé in being stitched over two horizontal threads, but gets its elongated shape from covering a single vertical thread (photo 2.14). Although it provides very little padding, it is quick to work. You can stitch the oblong cross on both types of canvas, but the most attractive result is achieved with penelope canvas. Take special care to keep your tension even on both diagonals of the cross. In addition to being very attractive for filling areas, this is a good background stitch.

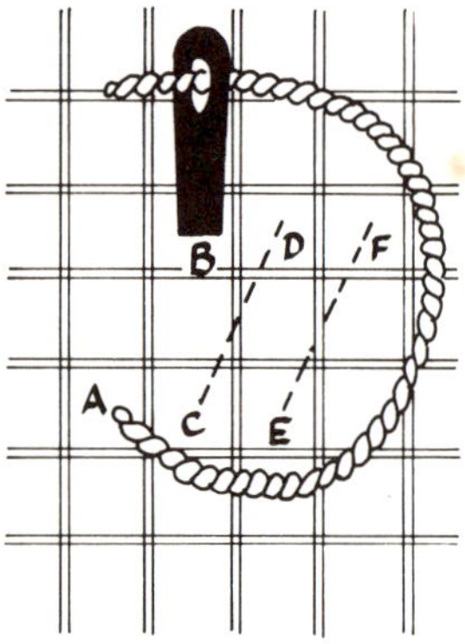

Fig. 2.28 Oblong cross stitch: making the first diagonals.

1. Bring the needle to the front of the canvas at A as shown in Fig. 2.28 and insert it at B, two threads above and one to the right of A. Return to the front at C, two threads directly below B. Insert the needle at D, as indicated by the dotted line in the illustration, and continue in the same fashion to E and F and so to the end of the row.

2. To complete the cross, bring the needle to the front at G, two threads directly below the top of the first diagonal of the last stitch and insert the needle at D, one thread to the left and two above G (see Fig. 2.29). Continue in the same way to the end of the row, returning to the front at E, and crossing the next stitch by inserting the needle at B, as indicated by the dotted line.

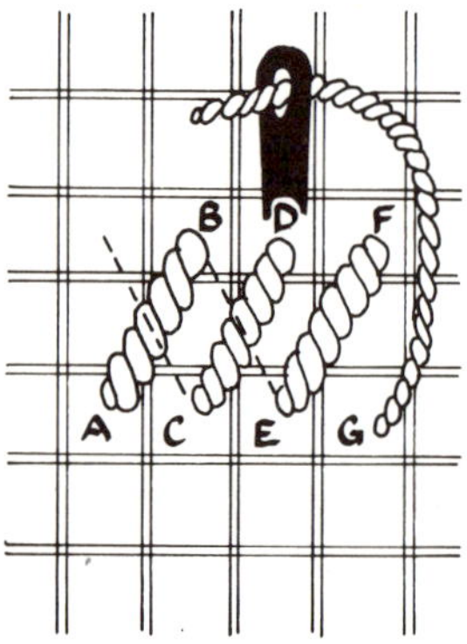

Fig. 2.29 Completing the oblong cross stitches.

Rice Stitch (William and Mary Stitch or Crossed-Corners Stitch)

The rice stitch (photo 2.15) is a simple cross stitch with each diagonal arm decorated to make a tiny cross stitch. It is of great importance to get the wool properly co-ordinated with the canvas size because the stitch can very easily look crowded and lose all its distinctiveness. This is another stitch which lends itself to many colour combinations; try working the main cross stitch in one colour and the small crossing diagonals in another. Each stitch is worked as a separate entity before moving on to the next one. It is slow to work.

1. Bring the needle to the front at A and insert it at B, two threads diagonally above and to the right, as pictured in Fig. 2.30. Complete the cross stitch by returning to the front at C, two threads directly below B, and inserting the needle at D.

2. Begin the next part of the stitch by making the stitches across each arm in the directions of the arrows in Fig. 2.30. E to F, back to E and down at G, to the front at H and back to G and finally to the front at H and back to F. Repeat these steps to make each stitch.

3. To work the second row, turn the canvas upside down and work exactly as you did in the first row (see Fig. 2.31).

Turn the canvas at the end of each row.

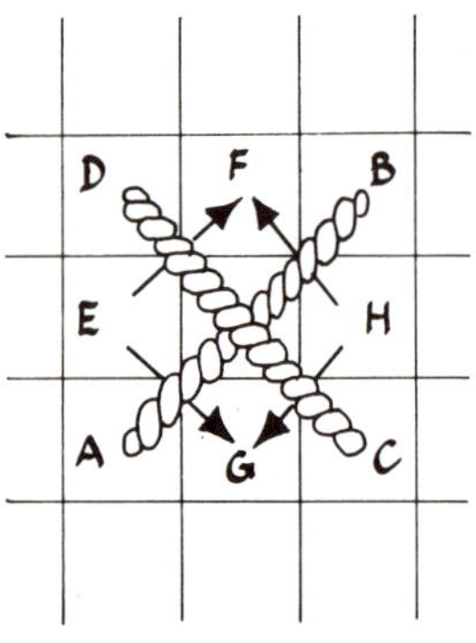

Fig. 2.30 Rice stitch: the basic cross. The arrows show how the small crosses are made.

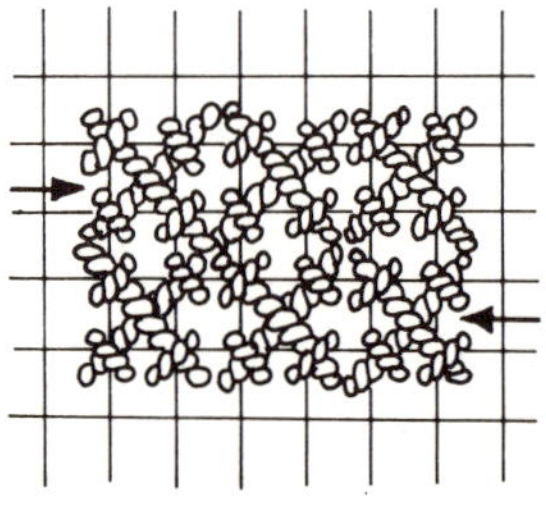

Fig. 2.31 Rice stitch, showing how the rows interlock. The canvas has to be turned for each new row.

Photo 2.15 *Rice stitch.*

Photo 2.16 *Double stitch.*

Double Stitch

This stitch is a combination of the basic cross stitch and the oblong cross stitch; the oblong cross of the double stitch is worked over three horizontal threads, rather than two (see photo 2.16). Each component of the double stitch is completed before the next one is started; therefore, be sure to cross each stitch in the same direction. This is one of the stitches that adapts very well to multicolouring.

1. Begin at A as shown in Fig. 2.32, and make the first arm of the stitch by inserting the needle at B, three threads above and one to the right of A.

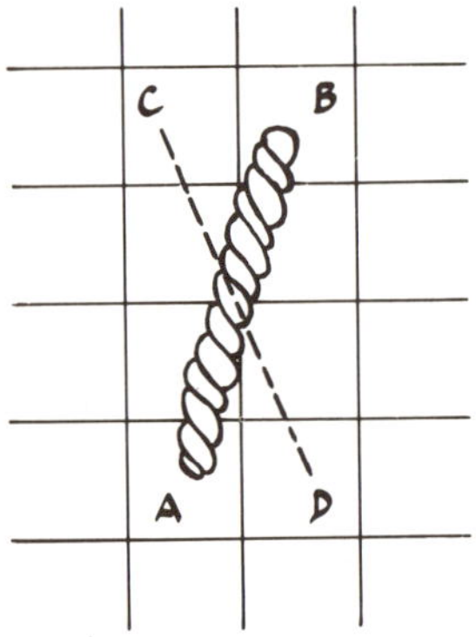

Fig. 2.32 Double stitch: the first diagonal of the oblong cross.

Return to the front at C, one thread to the left of B. To complete this part of the stitch, insert the needle at D, three threads below and one to the right of C.

2. To make the small cross, bring the needle to the front at E, (Fig. 2.33) directly above D, and insert the needle at F, one thread diagonally to the right of E. Come to the front at G, immediately to the left of F and insert the needle at H, directly below F.

3. To begin your second large cross, bring the needle to the front again at I, one row below H and insert the needle at J and coming to the front at K and returning to the back at L. Continue in this manner to the end of the row.

4. Work the second row as a reverse of the first row; begin with a simple cross stitch placed directly under the elongated cross stitch in the first row and fit an elongated cross stitch beside it, as shown in Fig. 2.34. Work all odd-numbered rows as you did the first row and all even-numbered rows as you did the second row.

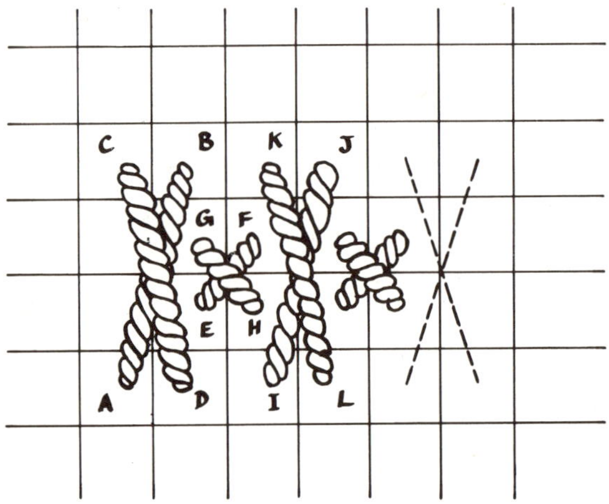

Fig. 2.33 Double stitch: the beginning of the first row showing how the oblong and basic cross stitches are worked.

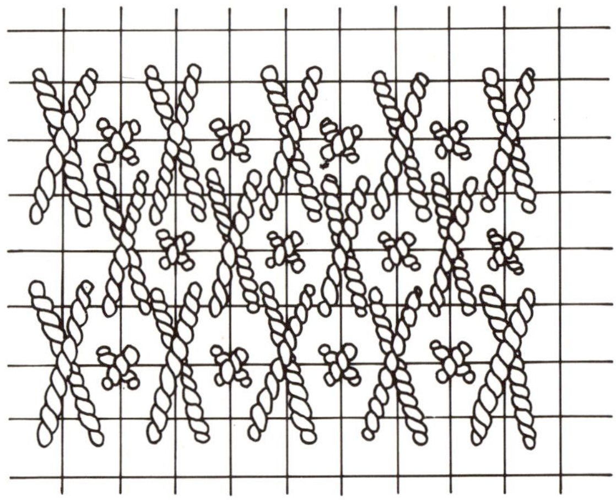

Fig. 2.34 The pattern made by double stitch is attractive, especially if it is worked in more than one colour.

Greek Stitch

The two crossed arms of the Greek stitch are of different lengths and create a very interesting effect in a design (photo 2.17). This stitch is quick to work and quite snag-proof, although it provides a minimum of backing. A good background stitch, its rows are worked alternately from left to right and from right to left.

1. Begin by coming to the front at A as shown in Fig. 2.35 and insert the needle at B, two threads above and diagonally to the right. Return to the

Photo 2.17 *Greek stitch.*

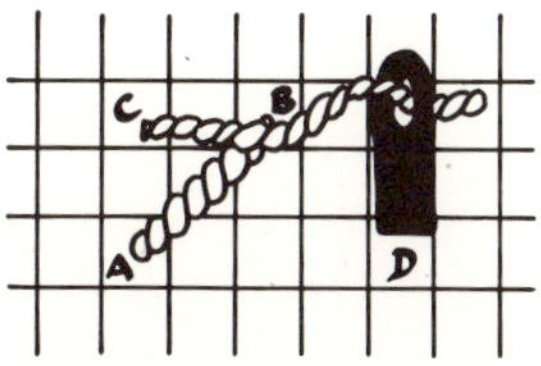

Fig. 2.35 Greek stitch; the basic cross.

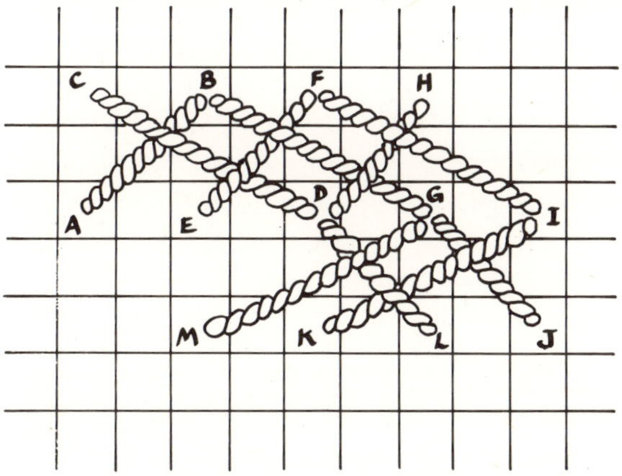

Fig. 2.36 Greek stitch: the beginning of the second row; note that this is worked from right to left.

front at C, two threads to the left of B. Complete the stitch by inserting the needle at D, four threads to the right of C and two threads below.

2. Begin the next stitch by bringing the needle to the front at E, insert the needle at F, and come to the front again at B (see Fig. 2.36). Complete the stitch by inserting the needle at G. For the third stitch, come to the front at D, insert the needle at H, return to the front at F and complete the stitch by inserting the needle at I. Continue to work in the same manner to the end of the row.

3. To work the second row (from right to left) bring the needle to the front at J, two threads below I, insert the needle at G, and return to the front at I. Complete the stitch by inserting the needle at K. Begin the second stitch at L and insert the needle at D, return to the front at G, and complete the long arm by inserting the needle at M. Fig. 2.36.

4. Work the third row and in the same fashion you stitched the first row, and the fourth row as you did the second, etc.

Photo 2.18 *Fern stitch.*

Fern Stitch

The fern stitch (photo 2.18) produces a very neat braid that is an interesting background or filler. It is quick to work and hardly distorts the canvas. This stitch can only be worked from top to bottom, so you will have to finish off your strand of wool before going onto the next row; if you do try to work down one side and up the other, you will find that there is no place to insert your needle. This stitch can be worked on both single and penelope canvas. The back of this stitch is well padded. When you include this stitch on your canvas, remember that each row requires three vertical threads.

1. Begin by making a small cross in a slightly different way from the basic cross stitch. Draw the needle to the front at A as shown in Fig. 2.37 and insert it at B, diagonally below and to the right. Return to the front at C, to the left of B, and insert the needle at D.

2. Make the first long arm by bringing the needle to the front at E, two threads to the left of D, and insert the needle at F, two threads below and two to the right of E. Return to the front at G, to the left of F, and insert the needle at H, two threads to the right and two threads above, crossing over stitch EF. Return to the front at I, one thread below E, and insert the needle at J, two threads below and two threads to the right. Return to the front at K, to the left of J, and insert the needle at L, two threads above and two to the right. Continue in this manner to make the next stitches (coming up at M and inserting the needle at N, coming up at O and inserting the needle at P) and then to the end of the row.

3. At the end of the first row, secure your wool at the back of the canvas. Fig. 2.38 shows how two rows of fern stitch fit together.

Note: Fill in with short diagonal stitches as indicated by the dotted lines in Fig. 2.38 if bare canvas shows at the ends of the rows.

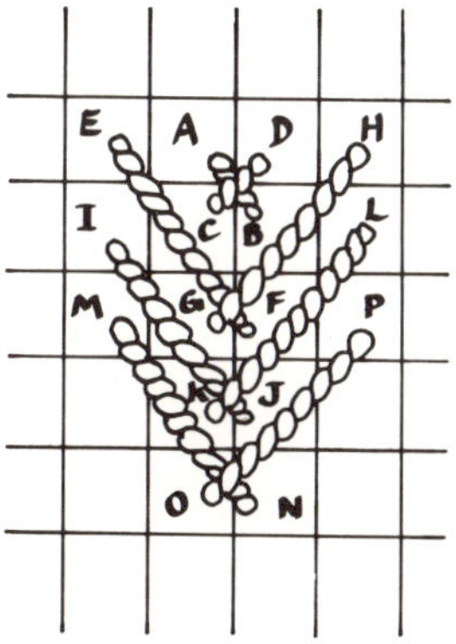

Fig. 2.37 Fem stitch is quick to work and makes an interesting background.

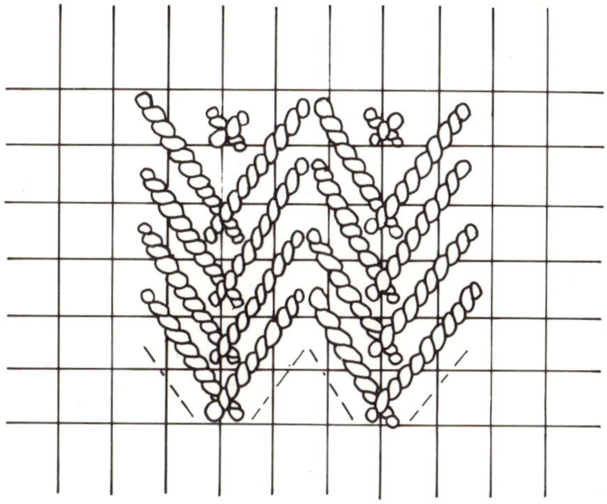

Fig. 2.38 This shows how the rows of fem stitch fit together. The dotted lines indicate fill-in stitches.

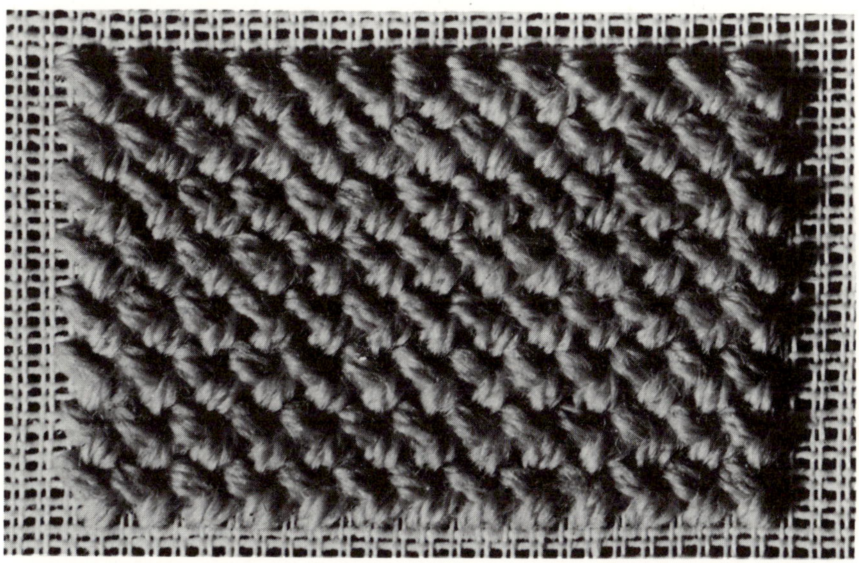

Photo 2.19 Herringbone stitch.

Herringbone Stitch

Stitched on large canvas, the herringbone stitch is worked very quickly and is useful for backgrounds and filling (photo 2.19). On fine canvas, working this stitch is a laborious task and it is best reserved for small spaces. In either usage, there is not much backing. The herringbone can only be worked from left to right; therefore, at the end of each row, you must finish off the strand and return to the left again, or you will lose the pattern. However, this does mean that the stitch lends itself very easily to multicolouring, and is especially appealing when alternating rows are worked in different colours. Tension is very important in this stitch. Although the herringbone can be worked on both types of canvas, it is better displayed when stitched on penelope canvas.

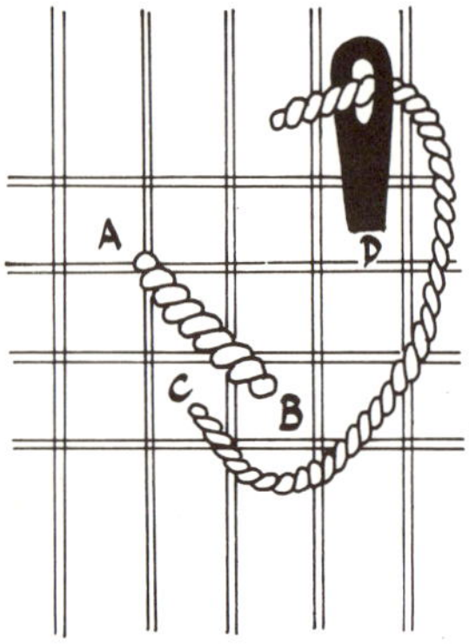

Fig. 2.39 Making the first herringbone stitch.

1. Bring the needle to the front at A and insert it at B, two threads to the right and diagonally below A, as shown in Fig. 2.39. Return to the front at C, one thread to the left of B, and complete the second arm by inserting the needle at D, in line with A and two threads above and to the right of C.

2. Begin the second stitch by coming to the front at E, one thread to the left of D, as shown in Fig. 2.40. Complete the stitch by going to the back at F, two threads below and diagonally to the right of E. Return to the front at G, and insert the needle at H.

3. To make the last stitch in the row, bring the needle to the front at I, one thread to the left of H, and insert the needle at J, two threads below and diagonally to the right (see Fig. 2.40). Cross this arm by coming to the front at K, one thread to the left of J, and insert the needle in L, one thread diagonally to the right of K and directly above J.

4. Cover all the bare canvas in a shape with the herringbone stitch and fit in individual cross stitches as indicated by the dotted lines in Fig. 2.41.

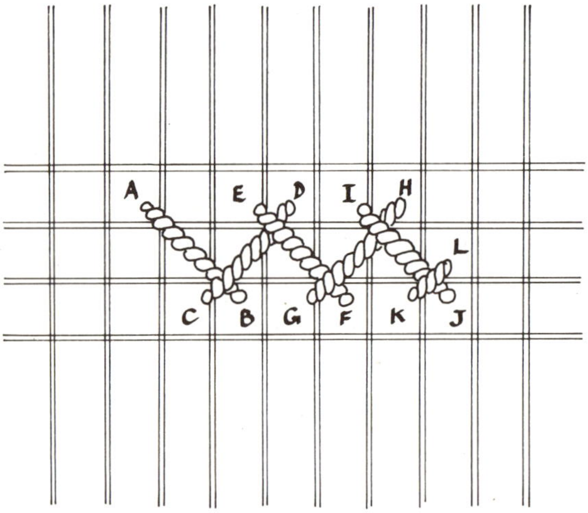

Fig. 2.40 Completing a row of herringbone stitch. Note the difference in the last stitch of the row.

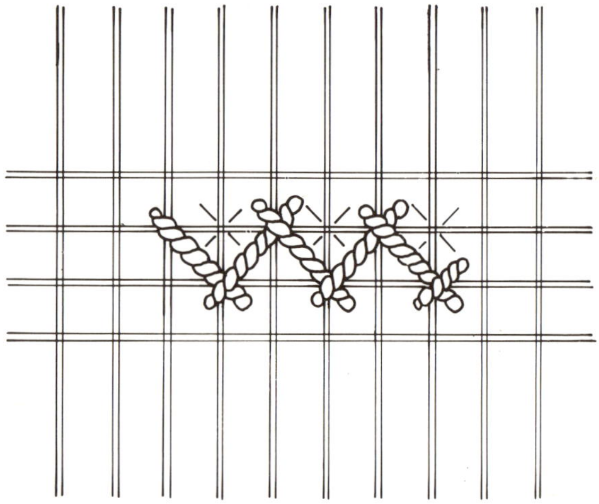

Fig. 2.41 Fit cross stitches in between the herringbone to cover the bare canvas.

Long-and-short Oblique Stitch

The long-and-short oblique (photo 2.20) is a long arm crossed by a short arm. When working this stitch, make all the long diagonals first from the top down to the bottom and cross them with the short diagonals working up from the bottom. Try creating an interesting effect by stitching the long and short diagonals in different colours. The long and short oblique is quick to work and provides a good backing. As you stitch the second and subsequent rows, be especially careful to place the needle in the proper hole and not to split the wool when stitching the short diagonals.

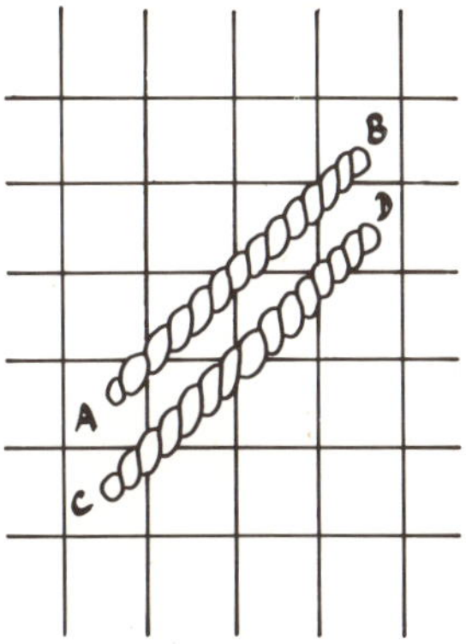

Fig. 2.42 When working long-and-short oblique stitch, work the long diagonals first.

1. Working from top to bottom, make a row of long diagonals by bringing the needle to the front at A, as shown in Fig. 2.42, three threads below the position in which you want the top of your first stitch. Insert the needle at B, diagonally three threads above A. Return to the front at C, one thread below A, and insert the needle at D. Continue to the end of the row.

2. To work the short diagonals, come up at E as shown in Fig. 2.43 and insert the needle at F, diagonally to the left one row above, thus crossing stitch CD. To cross the next stitch, return to the front at D, taking care not to split stitch CD, cross stitch AB and insert the needle at G. Continue in this way to the top of the row.

3. To make the next row, follow the number sequence in Fig. 2.44, coming up at the odd numbers and returning to the back at the even numbers.

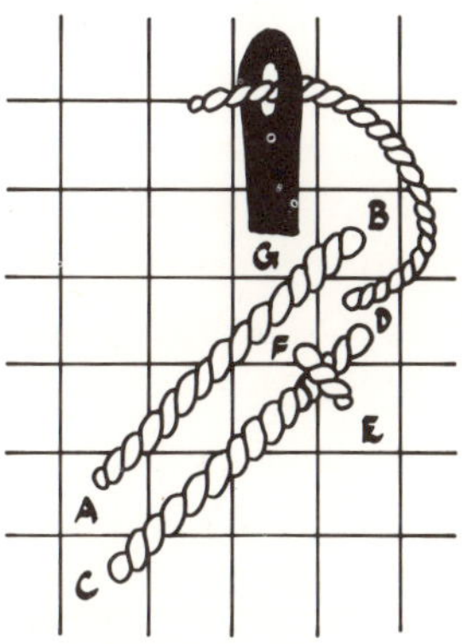

Fig. 2.43 The short diagonals of long-and-short oblique stitch look attractive when worked in a contrasting colour.

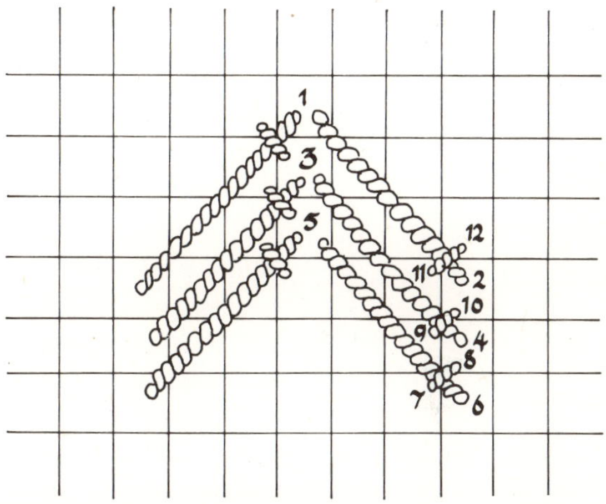

Fig. 2.44 This shows how the rows of long-and-short oblique stitch fit together.

Photo 2.20 Long-and-short oblique stitch.

Photo 2.21 *Mosaic stitch.*

Patterned Diagonal Stitches

Patterned diagonal stitches are a number of basic diagonal stitches, usually of varying lengths, worked in a pattern such as a square, rectangle or even steps. Each stitch makes a beautiful design in its own right, so there are endless opportunities for using them for emphasis in a pictorial design. The patterns are attractively displayed when you use the very simple technique of stitching them side by side in rows or geometric shapes; they also make interesting borders.

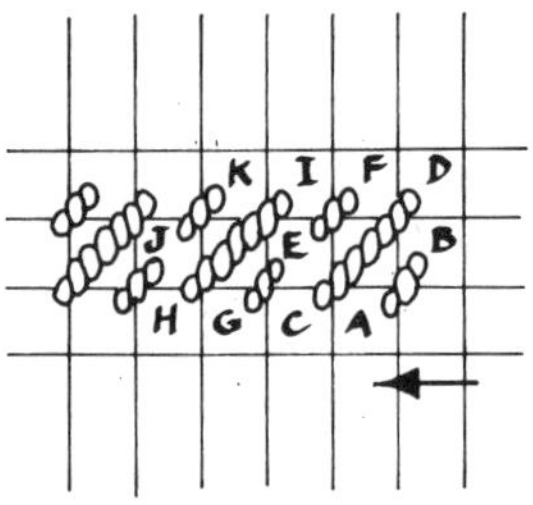

Fig. 2.45 Mosaic stitch is made up of three diagonal stitches worked from right to left.

Mosaic Stitch

The mosaic stitch is made up of three diagonal stitches worked over one, two, and then one thread to form a square (photo 2.21). Like the tent stitch, it should be worked from right to left, turning the canvas at alternate rows. The backing is durable, but the stitch does distort the canvas. The mosaic may be stitched on both types of canvas; and try working the stitches in alternating colours to produce a chequered effect.

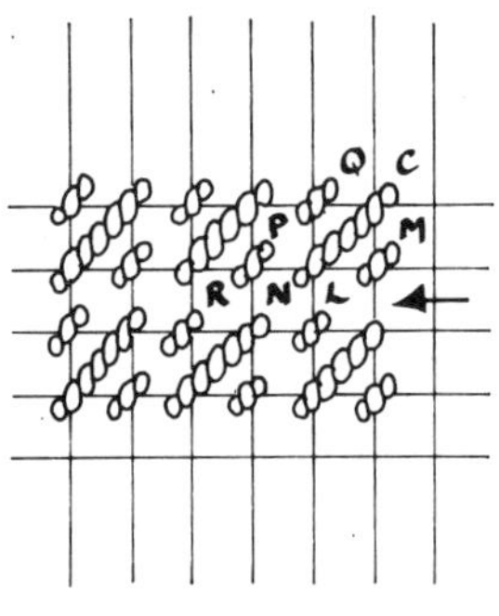

Fig. 2.46 Turn the canvas to work the second row. The pattern forms a series of squares.

1. As shown in Fig. 2.45, bring the needle to the front at A and insert it at B, one thread diagonally to the right. Return to the front at C, one thread to the left of A; insert the needle at D, two threads diagonally above C. To complete the square, come to the front at E, one thread above C, and insert the needle at F, diagonally above.

2. To work the second stitch, come to the front at G and insert the needle at E again. Complete the stitch by returning to the front at H, to the back at I, to the front at J and to the back at K. Continue to the end of the row.

3. To stitch the second row, turn the canvas upside down, as shown in Fig. 2.46, and work as you did in the first row, coming to the front at L, returning to the back at M, diagonally above, and returning to the front at N

for the long stitch. Insert the needle at O, return to the front at P, and complete the first square at Q. Begin the next stitch at R. Complete the first short stitch by inserting the needle at P again and continue to the end of the row.

Diagonal Mosaic Stitch

As the name implies, the diagonal mosaic stitch is the mosaic stitch worked on the diagonal of the canvas, this produces a striped effect and makes a fascinating background (photo 2.22). It is quick to work and may be stitched on both kinds of canvas. Like its relative, the diagonal mosaic has a firm backing; the rows are worked from the bottom to the top and the top to the bottom, without turning the canvas.

1. Begin at A as shown in Fig. 2.47 and make a simple diagonal stitch, to B. Return to the front at C, one thread to the left of A and complete the long diagonal by inserting the needle at D, two threads diagonally above. Complete the pattern by making the short stitch from E to F. This short diagonal doubles as part of the next pattern as well. Continue the pattern to the end of the row—coming to the front at G and returning to the back to complete the long diagonal at H, then the short diagonal from I to J.

2. The second row is worked from the top to the bottom in the same manner as the first. Begin at K as shown in Fig. 2.48, three threads to the left of the last needle hole, and make the first short diagonal to L. Return to the front at M and make the long diagonal to N. Continue to the end of the row from O to P, returning to the front at Q and inserting the needle at R, and so on.

Note: To cover the canvas completely, work a simple diagonal stitch over the threads that do not fit the pattern exactly. These stitches are indicated by dotted lines in Fig. 2.48.

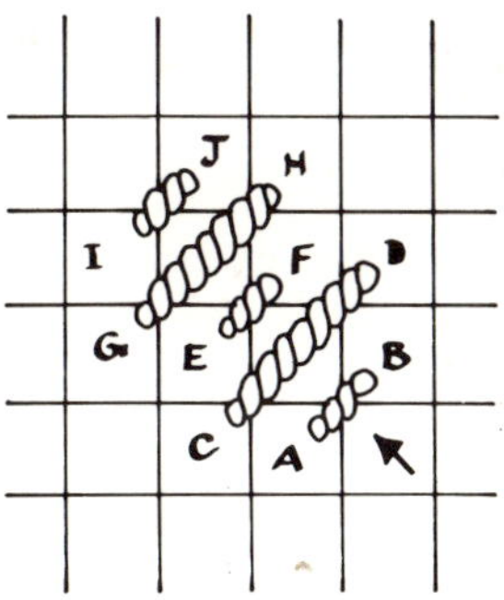

Fig. 2.47 Diagonal mosaic stitch is quick to work and makes a firm backing.

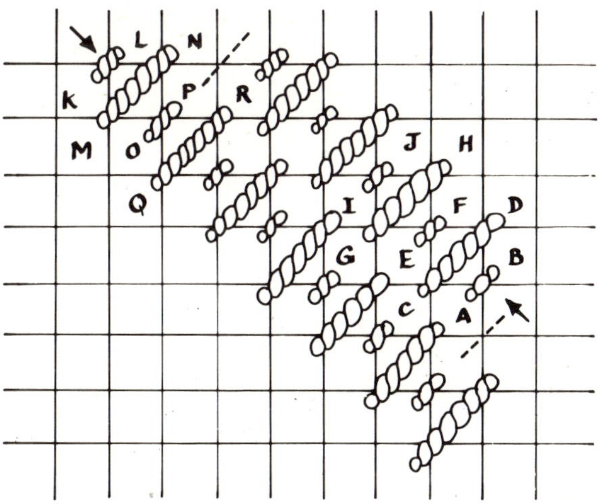

Fig. 2.48 Successive rows of diagonal mosaic stitch produce an interesting striped effect.

Photo 2.22 Diagonal mosaic stitch.

Photo 2.23 Scotch stitch.

Scotch Stitch

The Scotch stitch is also worked into a square pattern, consisting of five diagonal stitches worked over one thread, then two, three, then two again and one (photo 2.23). It distorts the canvas as it is stitched, but the backing is firm and durable and it is quick to work. The Scotch stitch may be worked on both kinds of canvas. Always work from right to left and turn the canvas at the end of each row. This is another stitch that makes a chequered pattern when stitched in two colours and makes an effective background, border or filling stitch.

1. Begin at A as shown in Fig. 2.49 and make the first short diagonal

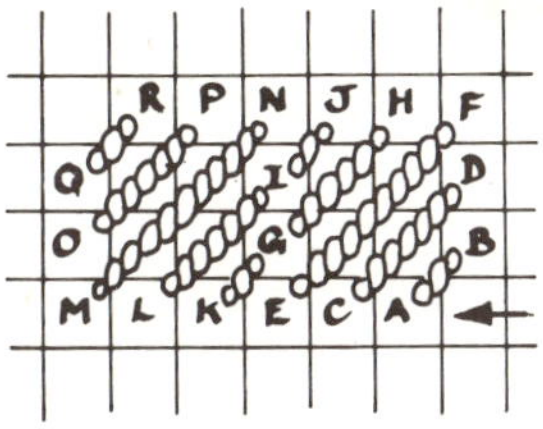

Fig. 2.49 Scotch stitch: the first row.

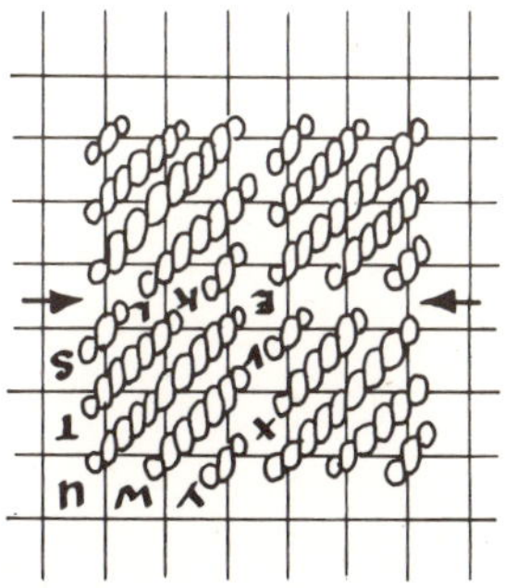

Fig. 2.50 Scotch stitch: the second row—remember to turn the canvas.

stitch over one thread to B. Return to the front at C and make the second diagonal over two threads to D. Return to the front at E and complete the longest diagonal by inserting the needle at F. Begin making the small diagonal again at G, one thread above E, and inserting the needle at H, two meshes to the right. Complete the pattern by returning to the front at I and inserting the needle at J.

2. Begin the second square at K, in line with A and one thread to the left of E. Make the first diagonal by inserting the needle at G again. Return to the front at L and make the next diagonal to I. Continue by returning to the front at M, down at N, up at O, then to P, Q and R. Complete the row.

3. Turn the canvas and work the second row as shown in Fig. 2.50. Come to the front at L and insert the needle at S; to the front at K, to the back at T. Work the longest diagonal by returning to the front at E and then to the back at U; return to the front at V and to the back at W. Make the final short diagonal from X on the front to Y on the back. Continue to the end of the row.

Chequer Stitch

The chequer stitch, a variation of the Scotch stitch, consists of alternating squares of Scotch stitch and tent (continental) stitch (photo 2.24). When worked, the chequer distorts the canvas but has a firm backing. It can be stitched on both types of canvas but is a bit slower to work than the Scotch stitch. Always worked from right to left, the chequer stitch requires six vertical and three horizontal threads for completion and it will require some planning to fit the full stitch into a design. This stitch is quite effective when worked in two colours and is best used as a background or border stitch. It also makes an attractive accenting stitch.

Photo 2.24 Chequer stitch.

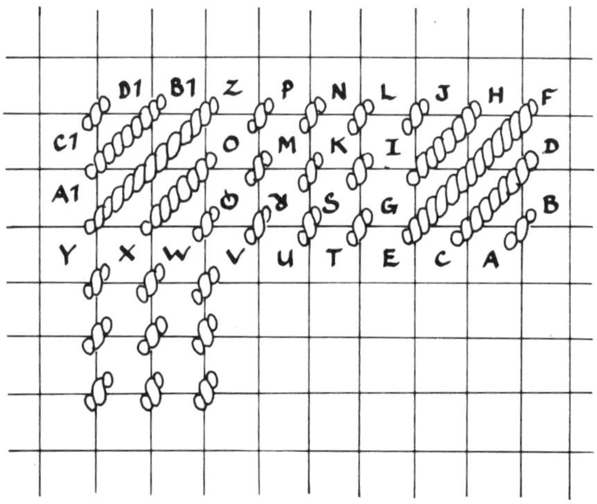

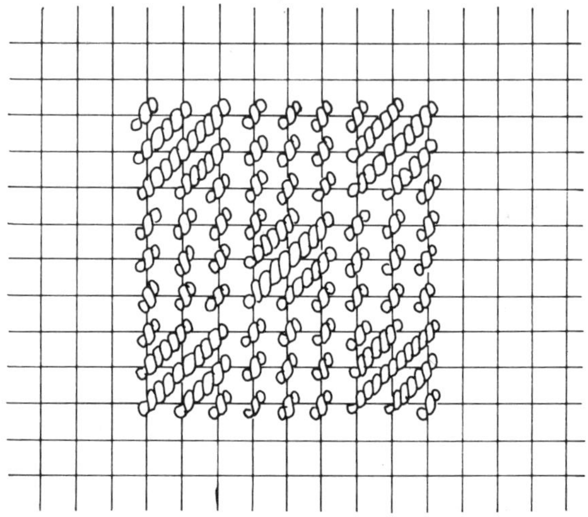

Fig. 2.51 Chequer stitch is a combination of Scotch stitch and tent stitch.

Fig. 2.52 Chequer stitch is effective when worked in two colours and makes attractive borders.

1. Begin by making the Scotch stitch as shown in Fig. 2.51, coming to the front at A, inserting the needle at B and so on to complete the stitch at J.

2. Work the second square of tent (continental) stitches by making three tent (continental) stitches to the left—come to the front at K, insert the needle at L; to the front at M and to the back at N; and to the front at O and to the back at P. Turn the canvas, and work three more tent (continental) stitches underneath these stitches—Q to M, R to K and S to I. Turn the canvas again and work a final row of tent (continental) stitches—T to G, U to S, and V to R.

3. Continue by making another square of Scotch stitch, starting at W to Q, X to O, Y to Z, A1 to B1 and finally C1 to D1; then another square of Scotch stitch, and so on.

4. In the next row, the squares are alternated again as shown in Fig. 2.52, a square of tent (continental) stitches under each square of Scotch stitch and vice versa.

Cashmere Stitch

The cashmere stitch (photo 2.25) is a rectangle of four stitches—two stitches each covering two threads, surrounded by two stitches each covering one thread. The entire stitch is two vertical threads wide and three horizontal threads tall. Always worked from right to left, it is a quick stitch to work and provides a good backing. This is another stitch that distorts the canvas, but, again, the distortion is easily rectified with blocking. The cashmere can be worked both on single and penelope canvas. When you include it in your design, be sure the number of threads running from top to bottom is evenly divisible by three and those in the width evenly divisible by two. This is another stitch that is very attractive if every other stitch is worked in a different colour.

1. Begin at A as shown in Fig. 2.53 and make the first diagonal stitch by

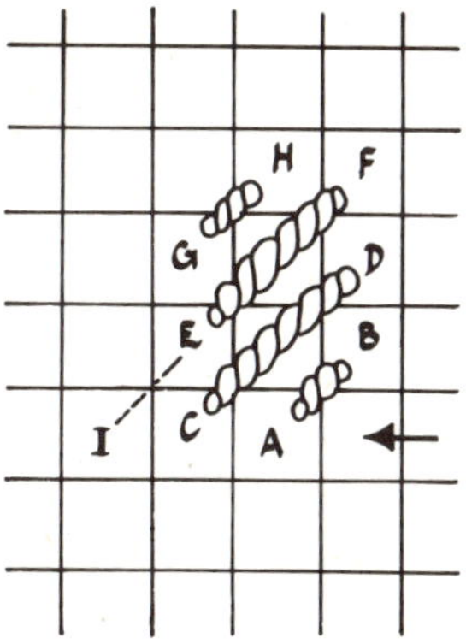

Fig. 2.53 Cashmere stitch is quick to work and makes a good background.

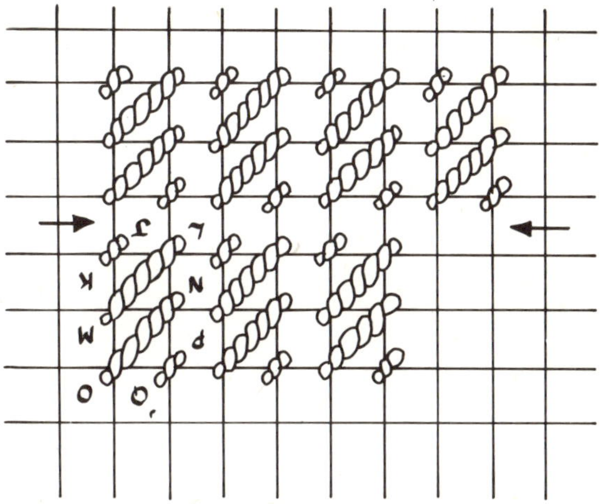

Fig. 2.54 This shows how the rows of cashmere stitch fit together. Turn the canvas to make successive rows.

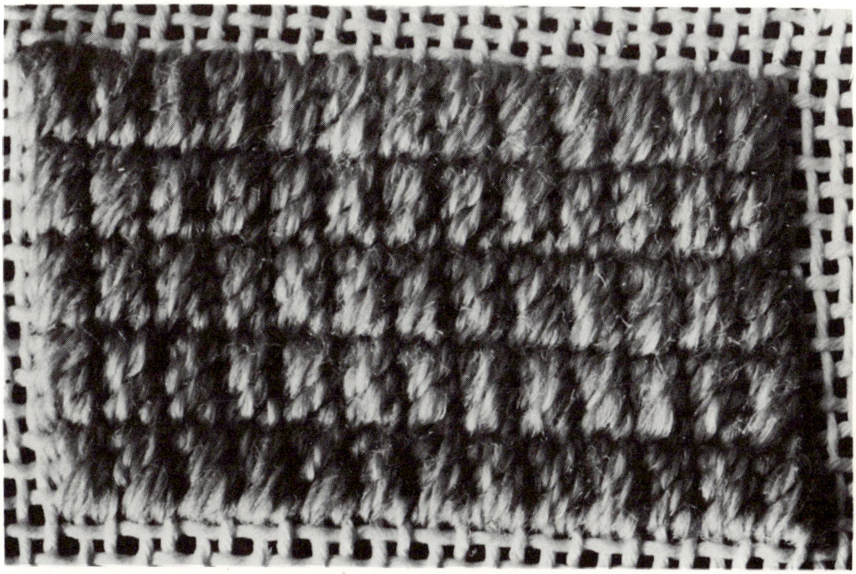

Photo 2.25 Cashmere stitch.

inserting the needle diagonally to the right at B. Come to the front at C, one thread to the left of A, and make the first longer diagonal by inserting the needle at D, two threads above and diagonally to the right. Come to the front at E, one thread above C, and make the second long diagonal stitch to F, two threads above and diagonally to the right of E. Complete the first stitch by coming to the front at G, one thread above E and inserting the needle at H, for the last short diagonal stitch.

2. To make the second stitch, begin at I as shown in Fig. 2.53 and inserting the needle at E, as indicated by the dotted line, Continue as above to the end of the row.

3. To work the second row, turn the canvas and continue as shown in Fig. 2.54, starting at J.

Photo 2.26 Milanese stitch.

Milanese Stitch

The Milanese makes a lovely pattern of triangles that alternately point up and down, giving the effect of brocaded fabric (photo 2.26). The triangles are made by diagonally working four rows of different length stitches—the first row consists of alternating stitches covering one thread and then four threads, the second row consists of alternating stitches covering two and then three threads, the third row consists of alternating stitches covering three and then two threads, and the fourth row consists of alternating stitches covering one and then four threads. The pattern is then repeated. Since the rows are always worked on the diagonal, you must start working in the upper left hand section of the canvas and work towards the lower right hand corner; then turn the canvas at the end of each row. Because of its lovely pattern, the Milanese stitch is most widely used as a background stitch. The backing is good and provides durability and the stitch is very quick to work. When this stitch is worked on coarser canvas, it becomes rather less snag-proof. The Milanese can be worked on both types of canvas but does have a tendency to distort.

1. Come to the front at A as shown in Fig. 2.55 and make the first diagonal stitch over one thread to B. Come to the front at C, five threads diagonally below B, and complete the second stitch over four meshes by inserting the needle at A. Come out at D and insert the needle back again at C to complete the row.

2. To make the second row of stitches (over two and then over three threads), turn the canvas and come to the front at E, indicated in Fig. 2.55. Make this diagonal stitch over two threads to F and return to the front at G, five threads from F. Complete the stitch by inserting the needle back to E and return to the front at H, five threads diagonally from E. Complete the row by inserting the needle back to G.

Above: Beads, different thicknesses and textures of wool and gold thread are combined in this panel. An exciting effect has been created in the sky by carefully letting some bare canvas show. Designed and stitched by Marion Poole.

Above right: This mirror frame is worked entirely in the leaf stitch. It measures 24 × 30 inches—the dimensions being selected to fit exactly over a hand basin. Worked by the author.

Right: The flowing design of this bolero was worked mainly in the upright Gobelin stitch. Designed and stitched by Bernard Berthon.

Right: This beautifully designed waistcoat is worked entirely in tent stitch. Designed and worked by Bernard Berthon.

Above: This shows the intricacy of the design worked on the waist-coat shown.

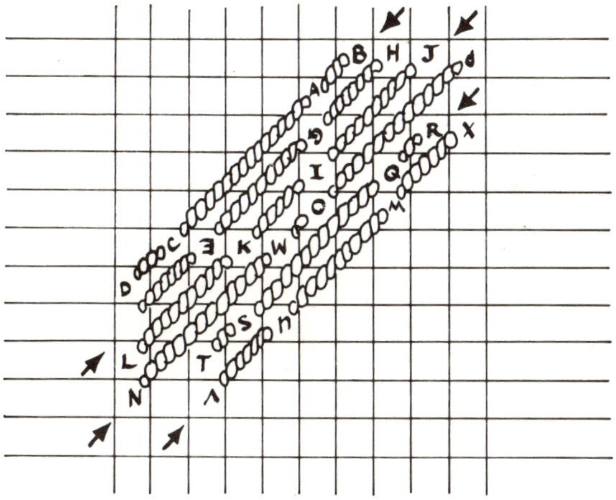

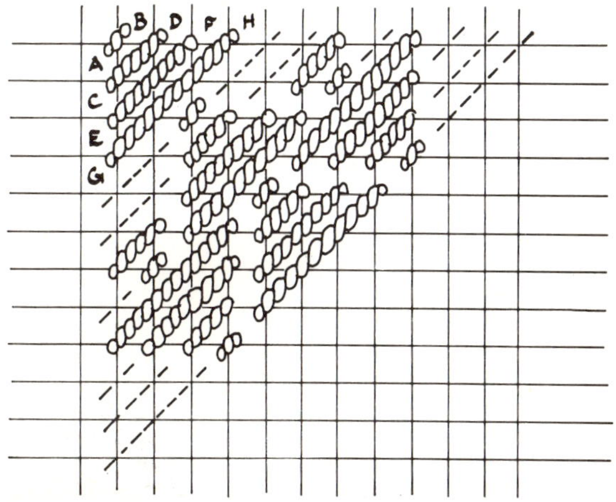

Fig. 2.55 Milanese stitch. Composed of triangles, this makes a very attractive background.

Fig. 2.56 Milanese stitch may leave bare canvas. Fill in with diagonal stitches that maintain the pattern.

3. To stitch the third row (over three, then over two threads), turn the canvas and come to the front at I, one thread below G and insert the needle back to J, three threads diagonally above. Return to the front at K and make the second diagonal, over two threads back to I. Return to the front at L and complete the final back stitch over three meshes to K.

4. To work the fourth row (over four, then over one thread), turn the canvas, come to the front at M, beside K, and insert the needle back to N, four threads diagonally from M. Come to the front at O, five threads from N, for the first short stitch of the row. Insert the needle back to M. Return to the front at P, five threads diagonally from M, and complete the pattern by inserting the needle at O.

5. From here, the stitch pattern repeats itself—not from the edge of the canvas, but on the diagonal. Therefore, the point of the next triangle does not start at the edge of the canvas as expected, but diagonally in line with the first point, A. Turn the canvas, and come to the front at Q, three threads below and two to the left of P, to make the first stitch over one thread back to R. (For the moment, do not worry about the bare canvas; you are just practising this stitch to get the rhythm.) Return to the front at S and make the next stitch over four threads back to Q. Come to the front at T and make the next stitch back to S, over one thread.

6. Turn the canvas to work the second row of this pattern. Come to the front at U, insert the needle back to V, come to the front at W and insert the needle back to U, come to the front at X and insert the needle back to W. Turn the canvas and continue until you have mastered the rhythm.

Note: To cover the bare canvas where the stitches do not exactly conform to the pattern, simply fill in with diagonal stitches that best maintain the pattern. To begin in a corner, see Fig. 2.56. The dotted lines indicate fill-in stitches.

Byzantine Stitch

Another stitch that has a brocaded pattern, and is useful for backgrounds, is the Byzantine stitch (photo 2.27). It consists of diagonal stitches worked in a step pattern and is quick to work and has a good backing. This stitch distorts the canvas and is best worked on single canvas but it does lend itself very well to multicolouring. There are a number of ways to work the Byzantine. First, the steps may start from left to right or right to left. Second, you can increase the width of the stitch without altering the height so that the steps become less steep. Finally, the individual diagonal stitches may be worked over either three or four threads.

1. The first four stitches are made across the canvas. Come to the front at A as shown in Fig. 2.57. Insert the needle at B, four threads above and to the

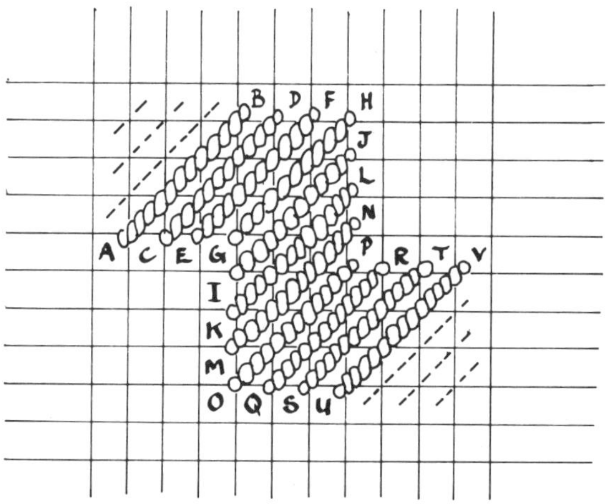

Fig. 2.57 Byzantine stitch has a brocaded pattern and is quite easy to work. Fill in with diagonal stitches as necessary.

Photo 2.27 Byzantine stitch.

right. Come to the front at C, one thread to the right of A, and insert the needle at D, beside B. Come to the front at E, beside C, and insert the needle at F, four threads above and to the right. Return to the front at G, beside E, and insert the needle at H, four threads above and to the right.

2. The next four stitches are made down the canvas. Come to the front at I, one thread below G, and go to the back at J, four threads above and to the right. Make the next three stitches below stitch IJ, coming up at K and inserting the needle at L, coming up at M and inserting the needle at N, coming up at O and inserting the needle at P.

3. The next four stitches are worked across the canvas and the next four worked downwards. Continue the pattern in this fashion to the end of the row.

4. Fit all subsequent rows alongside the first row, and fill in the bare canvas with diagonal stitches as indicated in Fig. 2.57 by the dotted lines.

Jacquard Stitch

Well suited to background work, the Jacquard stitch is another with a step-like pattern (photo 2.28). It consists of two different sized stitches—one row covering two vertical and two horizontal threads and the next row covering only one. The result is very attractive and again somewhat resembles a brocaded fabric. It is not as quick to work as the Byzantine or the Milanese, but it does provide a good backing. It lends itself very well to multicolouring and is quite snag-proof. Although it can be worked on both types of canvas, the Jacquard is most attractively stitched on penelope canvas.

1. Begin at A as indicated in Fig. 2.58 and make the first diagonal stitch to B, two threads above. Come o at C, one thread below A and make the

Photo 2.28 Jacquard stitch.

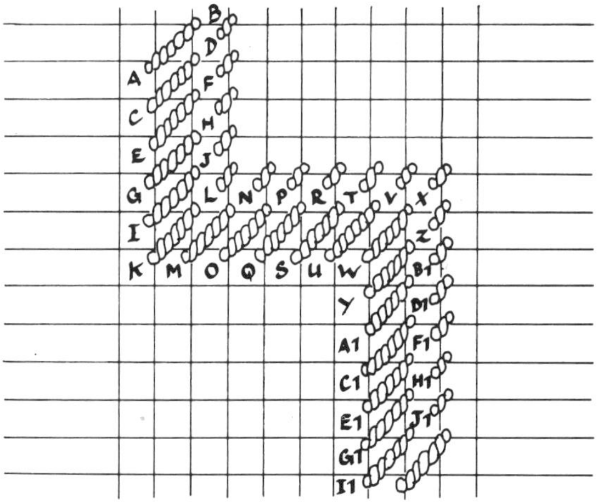

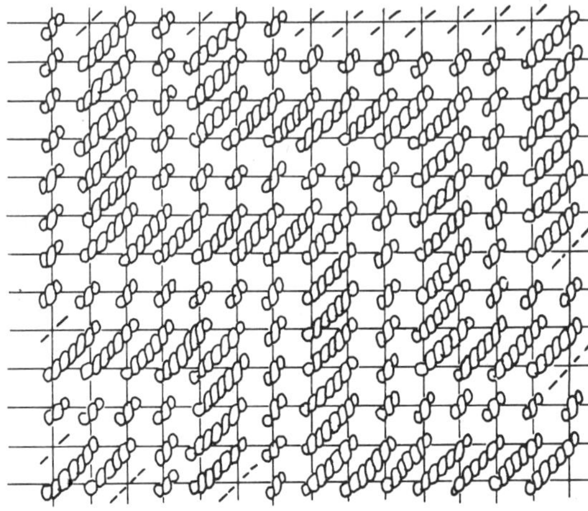

Fig. 2.58 Jacquard stitch is worked in a step-like pattern and lends itself to multicolouring.

Fig. 2.59 The Jacquard stitch produces an attractive pattern. Diagonal stitches can be used as fill-ins.

second diagonal to D. Continue until you have made four more (six in all), as indicated in Fig. 2.58, to stitch KL.

2. Make the next six stitches across the canvas by coming to the front at M, to the back at N, to the front at O, and to the back at P and so on to stitch WX.

3. Make the next six stitches down the canvas in the same manner down to stitch I1J1.

4. When you have worked the required number of long diagonals, turn the canvas and stitch a row of short diagonals, covering one thread, beside the long diagonals, as indicated in Fig. 2.58. Continue the pattern by alternating rows of long and short diagonals in step-like pattern already stitched (see Fig. 2.59). Fill in the bare canvas with short diagonal stitches, indicated by the dotted lines in the Fig. 2.59.

Diagonal Stitch or Scotch Stitch done diagonally

Another step-like progression stitch, the diagonal stitch, is sometimes referred to as the Scotch stitch done diagonally. However, the diagonal is not stitched in the same way as Scotch. The steps are made up of various sized stitches that give it an appealing pattern that is well suited to filling small, plain spaces (photo 2.29). This stitch may be worked on both types of canvas and is quick to work.

1. Begin at A as indicated in Fig. 2.60. Insert the needle at B, two threads diagonally above. Return to the front at C, one thread below A, and insert the needle at D, three threads diagonally above. Come to the front at E, still in line with A and C, and insert the needle at F, four threads diagonally above. The next stitch, GH, is begun one thread to the right of E, at G and ends at H, three threads diagonally above. The next stitch is made over two threads: come to the front at I and insert the needle at J; this stitch both

Fig. 2.60 Diagonal stitch is quick to work and well suited to filling small, plain spaces.

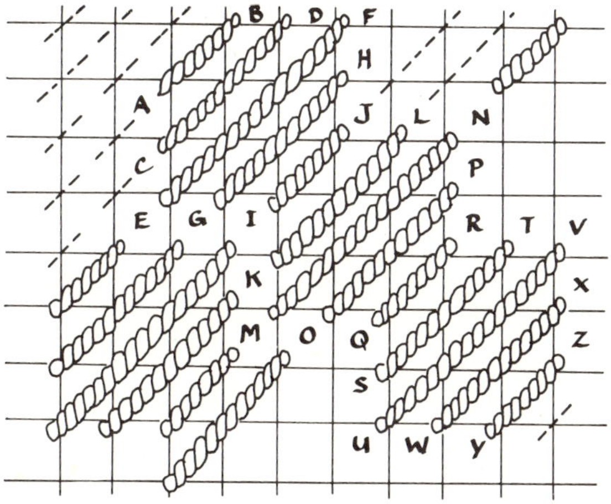

Photo 2.29 Diagonal stitch.

begins the next square and completes the first.

2. Come to the front at K and insert the needle at L, three threads diagonally above K. Continue to follow the letters until you have made enough stitches.

3. The other rows fit beside the first row, the shortest stitch of the first step in the new row beside the longest stitch of the neighbouring step as shown in Fig. 2.60.

Patterned Vertical Stitches

Unlike diagonal stitches, vertical stitches are worked straight up and down; it is therefore important that the wool fits the canvas very well, so that no bare canvas shows. The most elementary of the vertical stitches, the upright or straight Gobelin, is simply worked in straight rows, while the others, made up of carefully positioned individual stitches, create lovely patterns. Vertical stitches do not distort the canvas as diagonal stitches do and by combining vertical and diagonal stitches in one canvas you can create very effective contrasts.

Upright or Straight Gobelin Stitch

The Gobelin stitch (photo 2.30) is a very old stitch, deriving its name from the French tapestries. Usually it is worked over two horizontal threads, but this can be increased to three, four or five threads. Of course, as the number of threads increase, so does the possibility of snagging. The Gobelin is quick to work, but remember to gauge your wool to the size of the canvas mesh, and, if necessary, add another strand. Useful as both filler and background, the Gobelin is quite flexible in that it can be worked in either direction. It is preferable to work this stitch on single canvas, although it can be stitched on penelope.

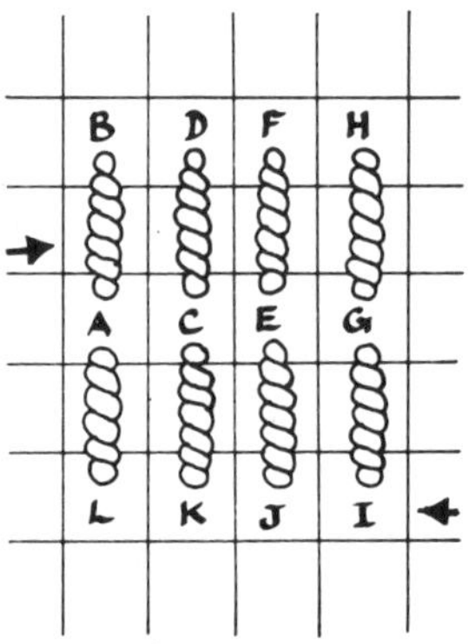

Fig. 2.61 Upright Gobelin stitch, one of the oldest French tapestry stitches.

1. Working from left to right, come to the front at A as shown in Fig. 2.61. Insert the needle at B, two horizontal threads above. Return to the front at C, beside A, and make the second stitch to D, beside B. Continue to the end of the row coming to the front at E, and to the back at F, to the front at G, to the back at H and so on.

2. Work the next row from right to left. Begin at I and insert the needle at G for the first stitch. Come to the front at J and insert the needle at E, shared with the stitch in the first row. Continue in this manner to the end of the row.

Note: If it is more comfortable you may, of course, begin the first row from the right and work the second row underneath it, from the left.

Photo 2.30 Upright or straight Gobelin stitch.

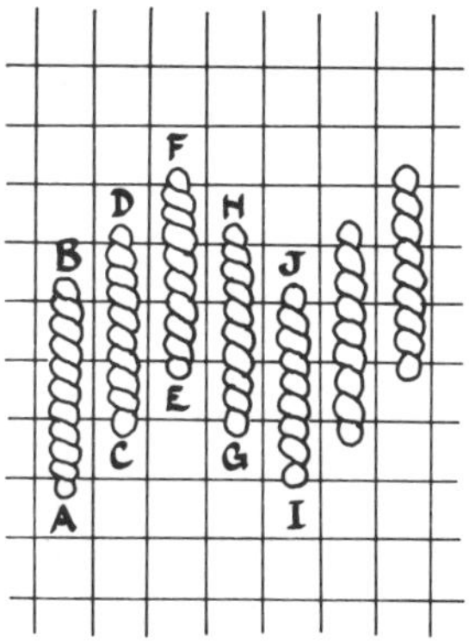

Fig. 2.62 Bargello (Florentine) stitch is traditionaly worked in shades of colours, but is also very effective in bright contrasting colours.

Bargello Stitch or Florentine Stitch or Flame Stitch

The craft of Bargello embroidery or Florentine canvas work, as it is also called, is worked in the Bargello stitch, a simple vertical stitch. The Bargello (photo 2.31) stitch usually covers four horizontal threads, but it can be worked over any number of threads from two to eight. The Bargello stitch is always worked in repeated abstract designs that are usually variants of irregular zig-zag (or 'flames') or geometric shapes that fit together (photo 2.32). The patterns are made by varying the size of the individual stitches and by working the stitches in step-like progressions (photo 2.33). The stitch does not distort the canvas, but is prone to snagging as the size of the stitches increases. Very quick to work, the Bargello should always be stitched on single canvas. It may be used as a border or an individual background (photo 2.34). It is traditionally worked in shades of colours, but is also effective when stitched in bright contrasting colours (photo 2.35). This stitch may be worked in either direction.

1. Begin at A as shown in Fig. 2.62 and insert the needle at B, four threads above. Return to the front at C, three threads below, and make the second stitch four threads above to D. Make the third stitch by coming to the front at E, three threads below D, and insert the needle at F. Come to the front at G, five threads below, and insert the needle at H, four threads above. Return to the front at I, five threads below, and insert the needle at J, four threads above.

2. Repeat this pattern all the way across the canvas. All the other rows are fitted above or below the first row, which establishes the design.

Note: Some Bargello patterns are somewhat complicated and require careful planning and measurement to ensure that you start in the right place so that the pattern is centred. However, once you have mastered the first row, all the others follow automatically.

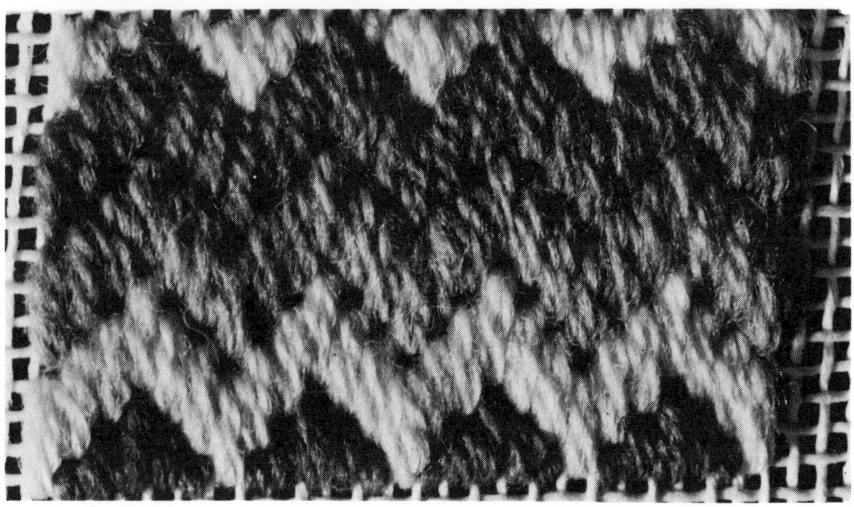

Photo 2.31 Bargello stitch.

Photo 2.32 Florentine (Bargello) stitched piece worked during the eighteenth century. (Crown copyright, courtesy of the Victoria and Albert Museum, London)

Photo 2.33 This piece, using numerous stitches around a Florentine (Bargello) stitched centre, was designed and worked by Miss J. Stevens.

Photo 2.34 The design of this piece is based on Exeter Cathedral, in the home town of the designer. It shows how effective Florentine (Bargello) can be when used as the background stitch. The beauty of the circular stained-glass window is highlighted by dark beads stitched on to the canvas. Designed and stitched by Eileen Bailey.

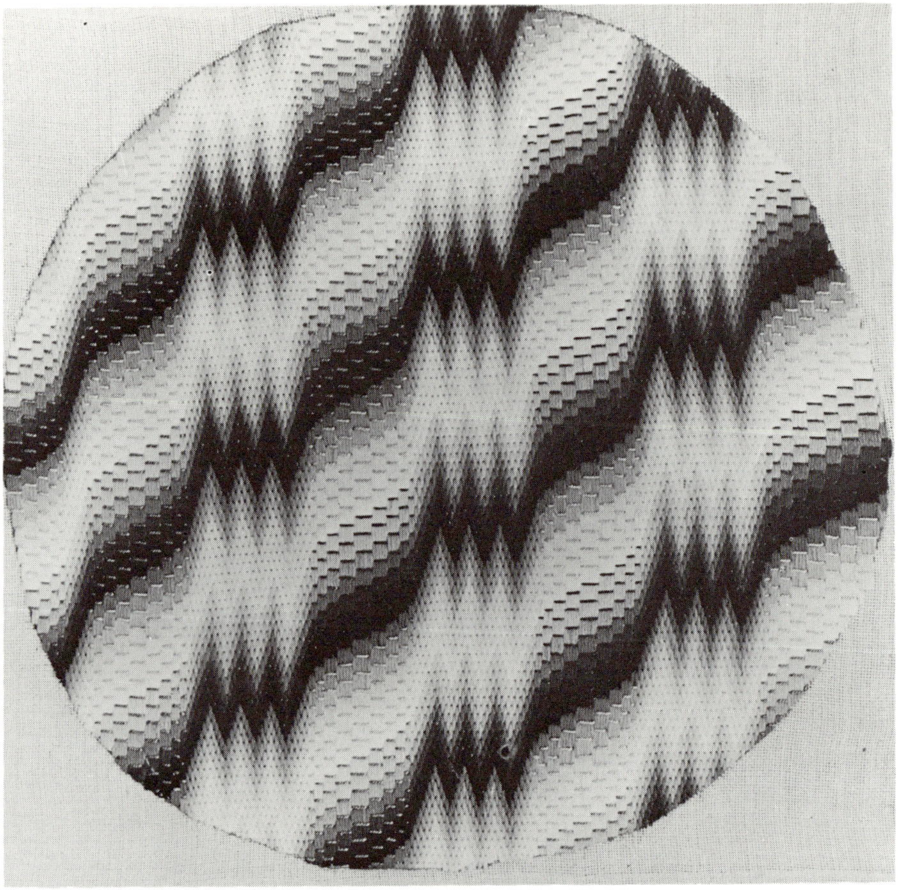

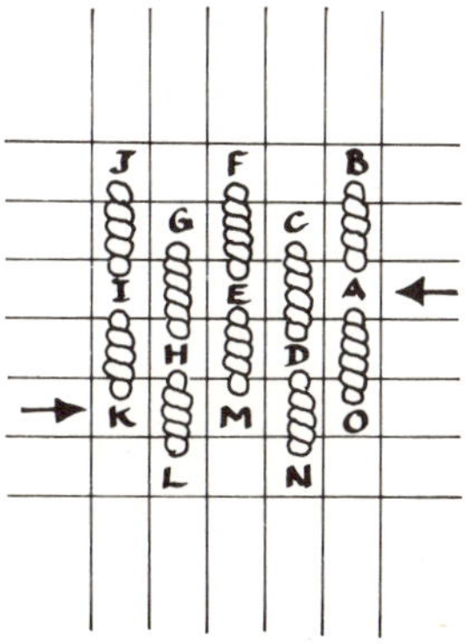

Fig. 2.63 Brick stitch is easy to work and makes an excellent background and filler.

Brick Stitch

As the name implies, the brick stitch makes a brick-work pattern (photo 2.36). Usually covering two threads, the stitch can also be worked over four threads, making the pattern larger. Quick to work, the brick should be stitched on single canvas. It provides an average backing and does not distort the canvas. You may have to add another strand of wool to cover the canvas completely, but in any case, be sure to keep the wool untwisted, and the tension even. The brick is worked from right to left and left to right without turning the canvas. The lovely pattern of this stitch makes an excellent background and filler.

1. Come to the front at A as shown in Fig. 2.63. Insert the needle at B, two threads above. Make the second stitch by returning to the front at C, one thread diagonally to the left, and insert the needle at D, two threads below. Come to the front at E, diagonally above and to the left of D, and insert the needle at F, two threads above. Come to the front at G, one thread diagonally below F, and insert the needle at H; return to the front at I and insert the needle at J.

2. To work the second row, come to the front at I and insert the needle at K, two threads below. Bring the needle to the front at H and insert the needle at L, come to the front at M and insert the needle at E, return to the front at D and insert the needle at N, come to the front at O and insert the needle at A.

3. Continue in the same manner, working all odd rows as you did the first row and all even rows as you did the second row. To make the edges flush, fill in with short vertical stitches.

Photo 2.35 This piece illustrates how Florentine (Bargello) patterns can be combined with other canvas-embroidery stitches. Designed and stitched by Lesley Moore.

Photo 2.36 Brick stitch.

Photo 2.37 *Parisian embroidery stitch.*

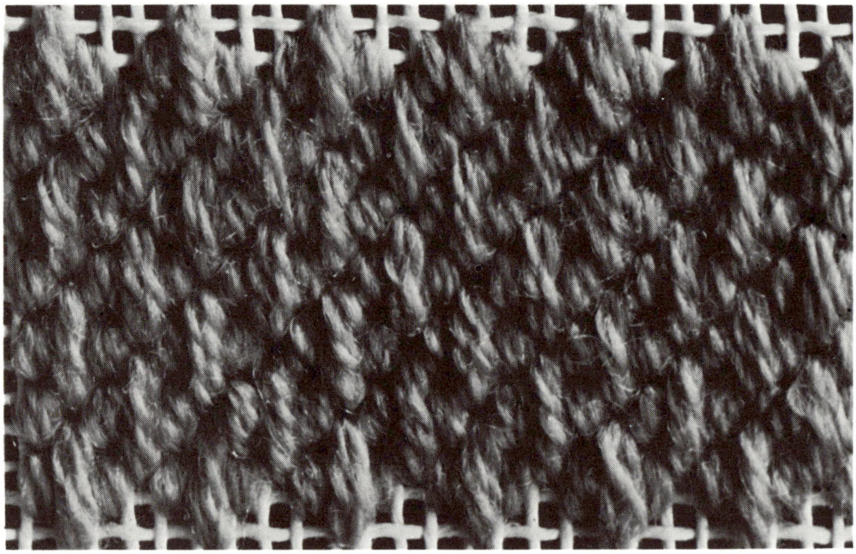

Photo 2.38 *Hungarian embroidery stitch.*

Parisian Embroidery Stitch

The Parisian embroidery stitch (photo 2.37) with its alternating long and short vertical stitches makes a charming pattern, especially if every other row is worked in a different colour. Best stitched on single canvas, the Parisian embroidery is quick to work and does not distort the canvas. The stitch uses wool economically, but the backing is minimal. You may have to add an extra strand of wool to cover the canvas completely, but always be certain to keep the wool untwisted. This stitch may be worked back and forth in either direction, without having to turn the canvas, and is excellent for backgrounds and filling.

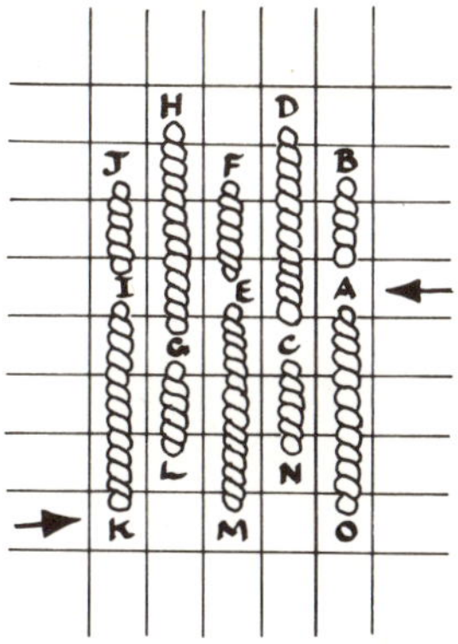

Fig. 2.64 *Two rows of Parisian embroidery stitch. This stitch is easy to work and the canvas does not have to be turned for each row.*

1. Working from right to left, come to the front at A as shown in Fig. 2.64 and make the first short stitch to B, two threads above. Return to the front at C, one thread diagonally below A, make the first long stitch to D, four threads above C. Return to the front at E, one thread diagonally above C, for the second short stitch to F, two threads above. Return to the front at G, one thread diagonally below E, and insert the needle at H, four threads above. Come to the front at I and insert the needle at J. Continue in this manner to the end of the row.

2. To work the second row (from left to right), the long stitches fit under the short stitches and vice versa. Come to the front at K, six threads below J, and insert the needle at I. Return to the front at L, three threads below I, and insert the needle at G, two threads above. Return to the front at M, three threads below G, and insert the needle at E. Come to the front at N and insert the needle at C. Come to the front at O and insert the needle at A.

Hungarian Embroidery Stitch

Another stitch that makes patterns with alternating long and short vertical stitches is the Hungarian embroidery stitch (photo 2.38). It lends itself very well to multicolouring, either in rows or in individual groups of three stitches. Quick to work, this stitch does not distort the canvas. Like the Parisian embroidery, the backing is minimal, and the stitch is economical in its wool usage. You may have to add an extra strand of wool to cover the canvas completely; always be certain to keep the wool untwisted. Perfect for backgrounds and fillings, the Hungarian embroidery may be worked in either direction without having to turn the canvas.

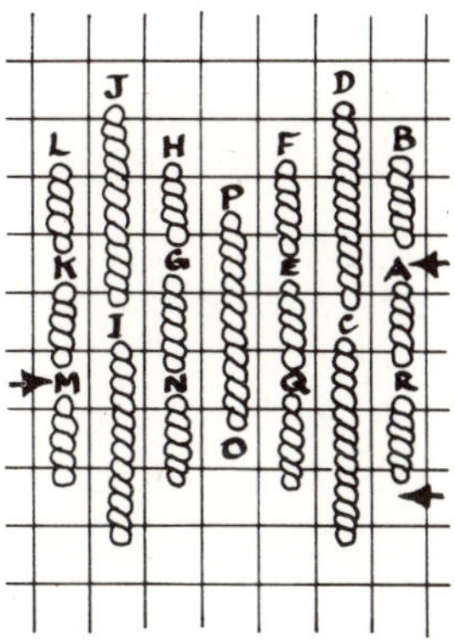

Fig. 2.65 *Hungarian stitch makes a pattern with alternating, long and short vertical stitches. It lends itself to multicolouring.*

1. Working from right to left, come up at A as shown in Fig. 2.65 and insert the needle at B, two threads above. Return to the front at C, three threads below B, to make the first long stitch to D, four threads above. Return to the front at E, in line with A, and insert the needle at F, to complete the first sequence.

2. The space between the next two vertical threads is left unstitched and the sequence is repeated by coming up at G, in line with E, and inserting at H, two threads above; returning to the front at I for the long stitch to J; coming up at K to complete the last short stitch at L. Continue in this manner to the end of the row, always leaving two blank vertical threads between each sequence.

3. The pattern of the second row fits between that of the first row with the long stitch worked between the two bare vertical threads. The sequence remains short, long, short, space, but at the beginning of a row you may have to start in the middle of the sequence. Come to the front at M and insert the needle at K, forming the last short stitch of a sequence. Skip the next two vertical threads and begin the next sequence by coming up at N and inserting the needle at G. Come to the front at O, for the long stitch, and

insert the needle at P, four threads above (this stitch will be half in the first row and half in the second row). Come to the front at Q and insert the needle at E, two threads above, to complete the sequence. Leave the next two vertical threads blank and begin the next pattern with a short stitch, coming up at R and inserting the needle at A.

4. The third and all subsequent odd rows are worked the same way as the first. The fourth and all subsequent even rows are worked in the same manner as the second row.

Note: To make the edges flush, fill in with tiny vertical stitches.

Old Florentine Stitch

A third stitch that makes a pattern with alternating long and short stitches, the old Florentine consists of two short stitches and two long stitches (photo 2.39). Because the long stitches cover nine threads they are prone to snagging and the backing is not evenly padded, but the stitch does not distort the canvas and may be worked back and forth across the canvas without having to turn it. It is quick to work and lends itself to multicolouring. The old Florentine is an interesting background stitch and excellent as a filler and for emphasis, provided there are enough threads to accommodate the long verticals.

1. Come up at A as shown in Fig. 2.66, six threads from the intended top of the row. Insert the needle at B, three threads above. Return to the front at C, to the right of A, and insert the needle at D, three threads above, beside B.

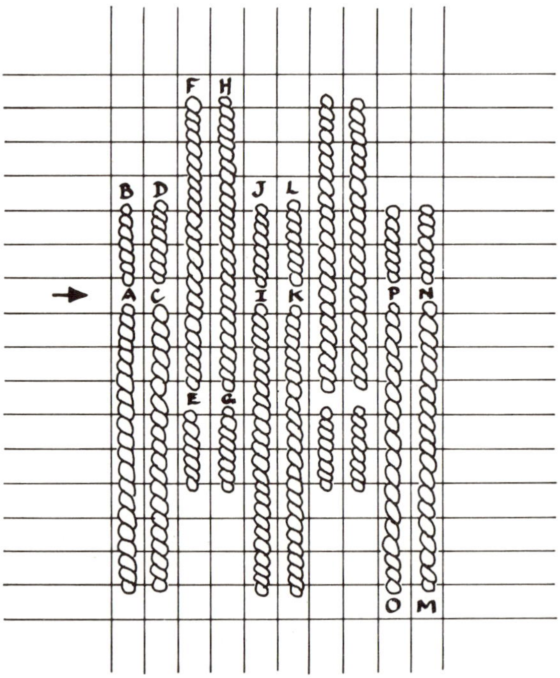

Fig. 2.66 Old Florentine stitch: an interesting background stitch and excellent as a filler and for emphasis.

Photo 2.39 Old Florentine stitch.

2. Return to the front at E, six threads below D, to make the first long stitch to F, nine threads above. Make the second long stitch by returning to the front at G and inserting the needle at H, beside F.

3. Make two more short stitches: return to the front at I, six threads below H and in line with C, and insert the needle at J; come up at K and insert the needle at L. Continue in this way to the end of the row, alternating two long and then two short stitches as shown in the Fig. 2.66.

4. In the second row, the long stitches are worked under the short stitches in the first row. Come up at M and insert the needle at N, nine threads above. Return to the front at O, beside M, and insert the needle at P, nine threads above, for the second long vertical. Continue the pattern to the end of the row.

5. The third row and all subsequent odd rows are worked in the same manner as the first; the fourth row and all subsequent even rows are worked in the same way as the second.

Patterned Horizontal Stitches

As a group, horizontal stitches have been unfairly ignored in modern canvas embroidery. It may be that the diagonal and vertical stitches are so widely practised that only recently have embroiderers wanted the challenge of a different type of stitch. The scope for working horizontal stitches in patterns, accented with different colours, is boundless; it is just as easy to vary a horizontal stitch and create a new stitch as it is to adapt a vertical stitch, so do try it. In fact, two of the stitches in this section have been created this way—simply by taking the wool to the canvas and experimenting. Patterned horizontal stitches make a lovely background and are just as attractive either as a filler or worked separately. They are usually quick to work, and do not distort the canvas. In the case of these stitches it is

Photo 2.40 *Horizontal Gobelin stitch.*

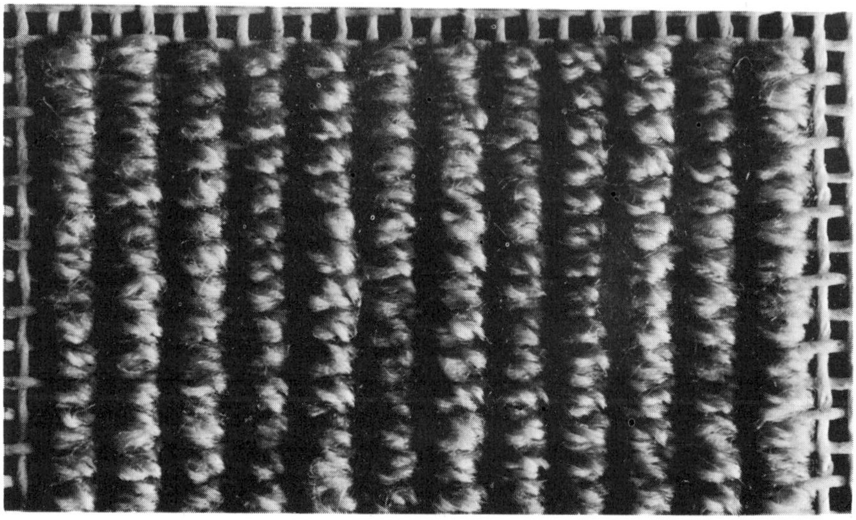

especially important that the wool should fit the canvas properly. Therefore, you are well advised to use crewel wool because it is easy to alter its thickness. Stitch carefully so that the tension is not too tight or bare threads will show through.

Horizontal Gobelin Stitch

Traditionally, the Gobelin stitch is worked vertically or diagonally; however it is equally attractive when worked horizontally (photo 2.40). The stitch may cover from two to five threads, but loses its snag-proofness as the number of threads increases. As with most horizontal stitches, you should keep the wool untwisted and may have to add an extra strand for maximum coverage. The best results are achieved on single canvas, which the stitch does not distort. It is quick to work and thus makes an excellent background stitch and a very effective filler. When using this stitch in a design, remember that it requires at least two vertical threads for each row. This stitch is worked from the top to the bottom of the canvas and back again without necessitating turning.

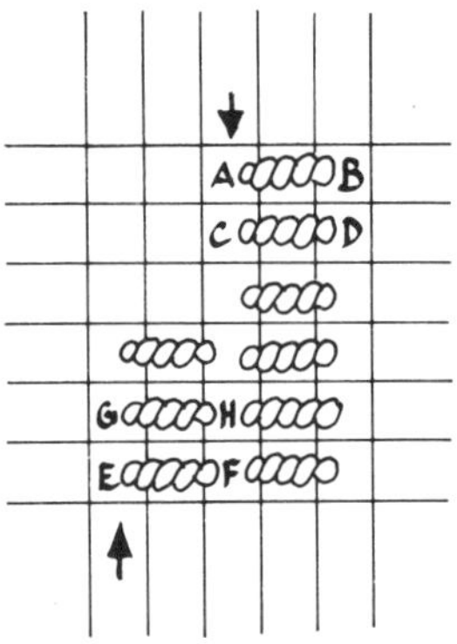

Fig. 2.67 Horizontal Gobelin stitch. The first row and the beginning of the second row.

1. Begin by coming up at A, as shown in Fig. 2.67 and insert the needle at B, two threads to the right. Return to the front at C, one thread below A, and insert the needle at D, two threads to the right of C and one thread below B. Continue in the same manner to the end of the row as indicated in Fig. 2.67.
2. To work the second row, come up at E, two threads to the left of the last stitch in the first row, and insert the needle at F, shared with the last stitch. Return to the front at G, one thread above E, and insert the needle at H, two threads to the right and shared with the corresponding stitch in the first row. Continue to the end of the row.
3. Work all subsequent rows alternately up and down the canvas.

Photo 2.41 Horizontal brick stitch.

Horizontal Brick Stitch

A simple adaptation of the very popular brick stitch, the horizontal brick stitch makes a similar lovely pattern (photo 2.41). The size of the stitch can be increased from the usual two to four threads, but becomes less snag-proof. This stitch is best worked on single canvas and does not distort. Again, you will have to gauge your wool to the canvas and may have to add another strand. Always keep the wool untwisted and the tension even for maximum coverage. This stitch is worked from the top to the bottom of the canvas and back again without having to turn. It makes an excellent background and filler stitch.

1. Come up at A as shown in Fig. 2.68 and insert the needle at B, two threads to the right. Come to the front at C, one thread diagonally to the left of B, and insert the needle at D. Return to the front at E, in line with A and diagonally to the right of D and insert the needle at F, two threads to the right. Come to the front at G and insert the needle at H, in line with D and two threads to the left of G. Continue in this manner to the end of the row as indicated in the drawing to stitch MN, coming up at I, returning to the back at J; coming to the front at K, inserting the needle at L; coming up at M and returning to the back at N.

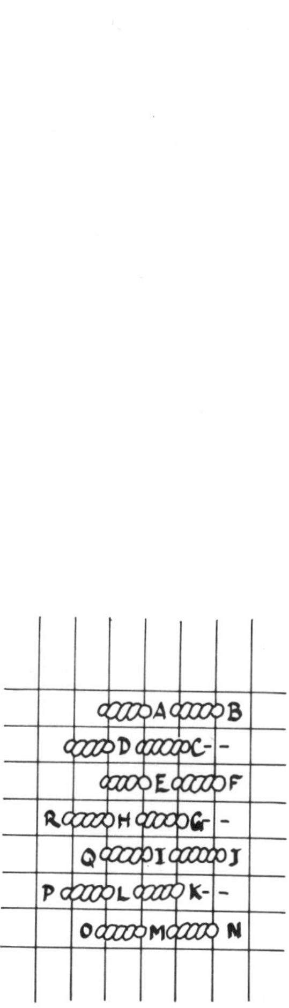

Fig. 2.68 Horizontal brick stitch is worked from the top to the bottom of the canvas and makes a good background.

2. The work the second row, come to the front at O, two threads to the left and insert the needle at M. Return to the front at L, diagonally to the left and above, and insert the needle at P. Return to the front at Q, diagonally above and to the right, and insert the needle at I. Come to the front at H and insert the needle at R, two threads to the left. Continue the pattern to the end of the row.

3. All odd numbered rows are worked in the same manner as the first row and all even numbered rows are worked in the same manner as the second row. Fill in the bare canvas at the edges with short horizontal stitches.

Horizontal Double-Parisian Stitch

The horizontal double-Parisian embroidery stitch was created by a friend of mine. The pattern is similar to the Parisian embroidery stitch worked horizontally, but with two alternating long and short stitches rather than one (photo 2.42). The most conveniently sized stitches are worked over two threads and then over four; however, we did experiment with stitches worked over four threads and eight threads and these worked very well but they are prone to sagging, especially on coarser canvas. Best worked on single canvas, the stitch does not distort; the backing is well padded, but not particularly firm. The horizontal double-Parisian embroidery is beautifully displayed when stitched in contrasting or shades of colours. You may have to gauge your wool to the canvas and add an extra strand for maximum coverage; be sure to keep the wool untwisted and the tension even. This is a wonderful background or filler stitch and makes a lovely design in its own right. It is worked up and down the canvas, turning at alternate rows.

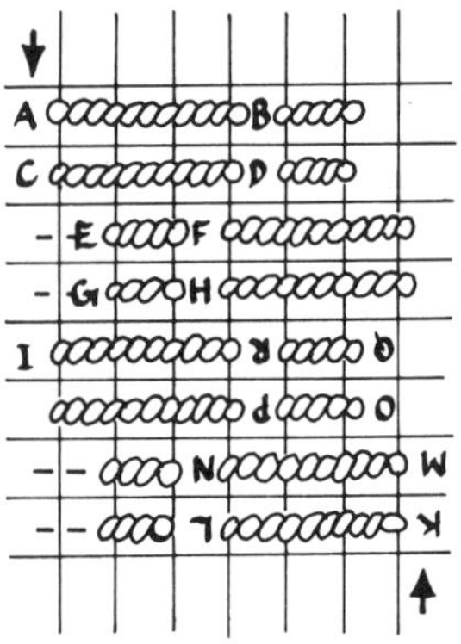

Fig. 2.69 Horizontal double-Parisian stitch: the first two rows. This is an attractive stitch when worked in contrasting shades of colours.

1. Come to the front at A as shown in Fig. 2.69 and make the first long stitch to B, four threads to the right. Return to the front at C, one thread below A, and insert the needle at D, four threads to the right, in line with B.
2. Come to the front at E, three threads to the left and one thread below D, and insert the needle at F, two threads to the right. Return to the front at G, below E, and insert the needle at H, two threads to the right. From here, the pattern is repeated. Come up at I, in line with A and C, and continue to the end of the row.
3. In the second row, fit the long stitches beside the short stitches of the previous row. Turn the canvas and come up at K and insert the needle at L, four threads to what is now the right (L is shared with the last stitch in the first row). Make the second long stitch by coming to the front at M and inserting the needle at N. Come to the front at O, one thread below and three to the left of N, and insert the needle at P, two threads to the right. Return to the front at Q, in line with O, and insert the needle for the second short stitch at R, in line with P. Repeat the pattern from here to the end of the row.
4. Turn the canvas at alternate rows and continue as above. To make the edges flush, fill in with horizontal stitches, as indicated in the illustration.

Note: If you find it easier to work across the canvas from right to left rather than left to right as instructed, you can do so. Follow the above instructions, but do not turn the canvas at the end of each row.

Straight Satin Stitch (two, four, six, eight)

This stitch (photo 2.43) is similar to mosaic diamond filling, a drawn-fabric stitch turned on its side. It consists of a series of horizontal stitches, varying in size and worked side by side to form a triangle. The individual stitches are worked over two, four, six and eight threads, and then back down through six, four and two; or they can be worked over one, three, five and seven, and then

Above: These handbags, cushions and tea cosy, designed by Bjørn Wiinblad, world-famous Danish designer, illustrate the adaptability of canvas embroidery to modern designs. These magnificent designs, with their pure, raw colours, are worked in cross stitch. Materials, chart and instructions (in English) are available from Haanderbejdets Fremme, Vimmelskaftet 38, 1161 Copenhagen, Denmark.

Left: Extending the length of the handles for this carrier bag to 32 inches (not including turn-under) will distribute the weight of the contents across the shoulders and make carrying heavy loads easier. The design is based on an Australian Aboriginal rock art, and the brick stitch, tent stitch and checker stitch were used. To protect it from rain and dust, the canvas embroidery has been sprayed with Scotchgard. Designed by the author and worked by Mavis McDonald.

Right: The design of this Christmas stocking is untraditional and unusual, yet well reflects the Christmas season. The design was inspired by folk stockings of Hungary and Scandinavia. Patterned stitches such as the Jacquard and Byzantine augment the theme while the cashmere stitch, worked in opposite directions beside one another, adds texture. The tiny wool bows were stitched in place after blocking. Designed and worked by the author.

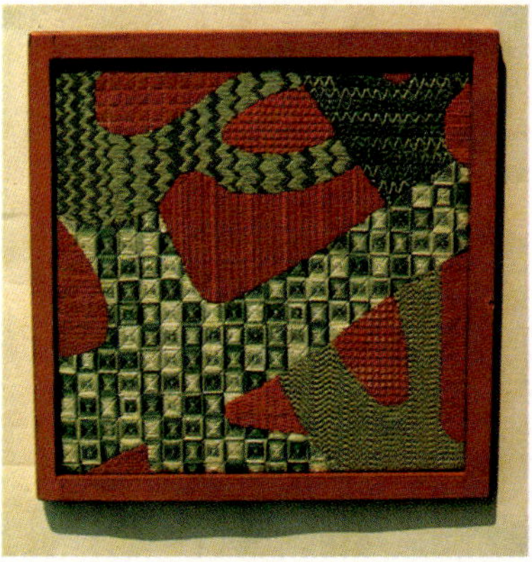

Right: This piece is another excellent example of the effect of combining other materials with wool in canvas embroidery. Varying the sheen of the embroidery cotton here has added texture and interest to the work. The rice stitch, the slanting Gobelin, the checker stitch and the brick stitch are among the stitches used. Designed and worked by Patricia Coles.

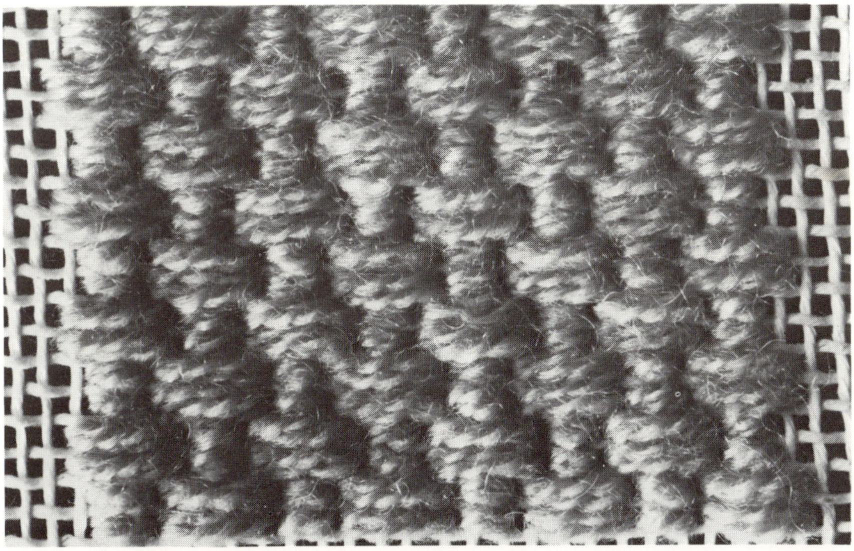

Photo 2.42 Horizontal double-Parisian stitch.

Photo 2.43 Straight satin stitch (two, four, six, eight).

five, three and one. In either case the longest stitch is prone to snagging when stitched on coarse canvas; however this is not as likely to happen if the stitching is done on 12 meshes to the inch and finer canvas. The backing is not firm but is well padded. This stitch does not distort and can be worked on both single and penelope canvas. The distinctive pattern of this stitch makes it suitable for backgrounds, borders and filling; and it is most effective when stitched in contrasting or shades of colours. As with other horizontal stitches you should observe the suggestions about gauging your wool and tensions.

1. Working from the top of the canvas, come up at A, four threads to the

left of the edge of your row as shown in Fig. 2.70. Make the point of the triangle by inserting the needle over one thread to B. Come to the front at C, one thread below and to the left of A, and insert the needle at D, three threads to the right. Come to the front at E, one thread below and to the left of C, and insert the needle at F, five threads to the right. Return to the front at G, one thread below to the left of E, and insert the needle at H, seven threads to the right. Stitch GH is at the centre of the triangle. Come to the front at I, in line with E, and insert the needle at J, five threads to the right. Return to the front at K, four threads to the left of J and in line with C, and insert the needle at L, three threads to the right.

2. From here the pattern repeats itself, the last stitch MN, over one thread, becomes the bottom point of the first triangle and the top of the second triangle.

3. In the second row, the longest stitch of the triangle fits beside the shortest stitch in the first row. Therefore, as shown in Fig. 2.70, come to the front at O, seven threads to the left of the last stitch and make the long stitch to P, covering seven threads. Come to the front at Q, the thread above and six threads to the left of P, and insert the needle at R, five threads to the right. Come to the front at S, one thread above and four to the left of R, and insert the needle at T, three threads to the right. Return to the front at U, two threads to the left and one above T, to start the next triangle; insert the needle at V, covering one thread. Continue to the end of the row.

4. To make the edges flush, fill in with horizontal stitches as indicated in the illustration by the dotted lines.

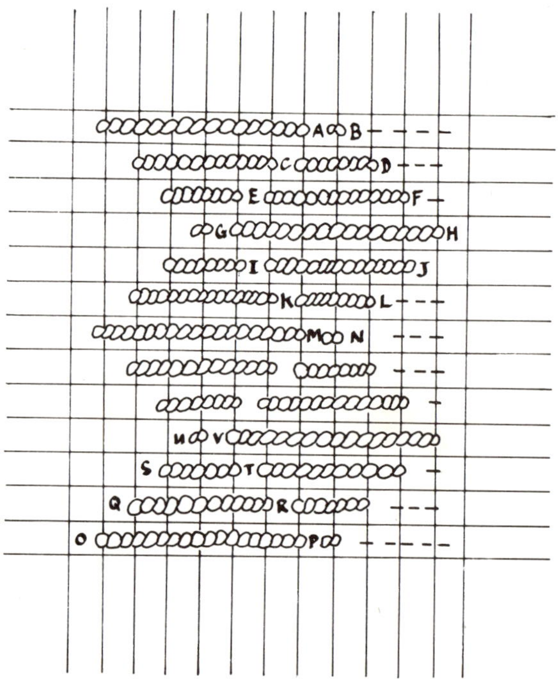

Fig. 2.70 Straight satin stitch (two, four, six, eight). This stitch has a distinctive pattern and looks well in contrasting shades of colour.

Photo 2.44 *Horizontal step stitch.*

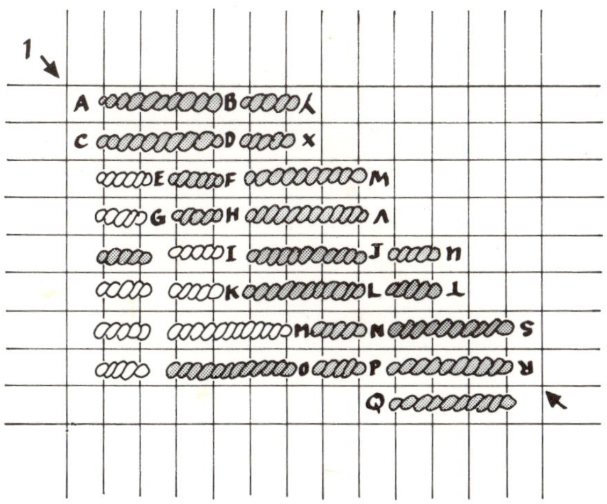

Fig. 2.71 Horizontal step stitch: good either as a border stitch or worked alone.

Horizontal Step Stitch

The horizontal step stitch is one that I adapted by experimenting. It consists of two stitches worked over four threads and two stitches worked over two threads and is worked in steps (photo 2.44). The backing is well padded, and slightly firmer than the straight satin or horizontal double-Parisian embroidery stitch. It should be stitched on single canvas and does not distort and its unusual pattern makes it excellent as a background or filling stitch. Like many patterned stitches, it is also lovely as a border or worked alone. The horizontal step lends itself very well to multicolouring. Again, gauge your wool to the canvas and keep it flat; always keep your tension even.

1. Begin at A as shown in Fig. 2.71. Insert the needle at B, four threads to the right. Return to the front at C, one thread below A, and insert the needle at

D, four threads to the right and in line with B. Make the two short stitches by coming to the front at E, two threads to the left and one below D, and inserting the needle at F, two threads to the right, return to the front at G, and insert the needle at H, below F. from here the pattern repeats; it is only the position of each sequence of stitches that changes.

2. Begin the second sequence at I, one thread below H, and return to the back at J, four threads to the right. Make the second long stitch by coming to the front at K, one thread below I, and insert the needle at L, one thread below J. Make the two short stitches by coming up at M, two threads to the left and one below L and insert the needle at N, one thread below L. Come to the front at O, one thread below M and insert the needle at P, one thread below N. Begin the next pattern at Q, one thread below P. Continue to the end of the row.

3. The long stitches of the second row will be worked beside the short stitches of the first row, the canvas having been turned. Begin by coming to the front at R, four threads to the left of P. Insert the needle at P, to complete the stitch. Return to the front for the second long stitch, at S, in line with R, and insert the needle at N. The two short stitches are made next; come up at T, two threads to the left of N, and insert the needle at L. Return to the front at U and insert the needle at J. From here the sequence repeats itself. Begin at V, in line with J, and make the first stitch to H. Come up at W, in line with V, and insert the needle at F. Continue to the end of the row.

Note: To make the edges flush, fill in with stitches as shown in the Fig. 2.71.

Combination Stitches

The stitches in this group are a combination of diagonal, horizontal and vertical stitches. Some combine only two types, while others are made up of all three. Most of the combination stitches cover the meshes or threads of the canvas more than once, which sometimes makes them slow to work but does give them a particular quality of texture which is quite attractive. In general, this group is most suitable for filling in and for backgrounds and some of the stitches are most effective for emphasis and as borders.

Knotted Stitch

The knotted stitch takes its name from a needlework term—tie-down—because its long diagonal stitch, over three threads, is tied down in the middle by a short diagonal (photo 2.45). Being tied down makes it quite snag-proof and hardwearing. The knotted stitch may be worked on both single and penelope canvas, but it does tend to distort the canvas if it is pulled too tight. Always worked from right to left; you must secure your wool at the end of each row and begin again on the right side of the canvas. This stitch can be worked by passing the needle under the threads of the canvas and up again in one motion, this makes it quick to work because you halve the number of

Photo 2.45 *Knotted stitch.*

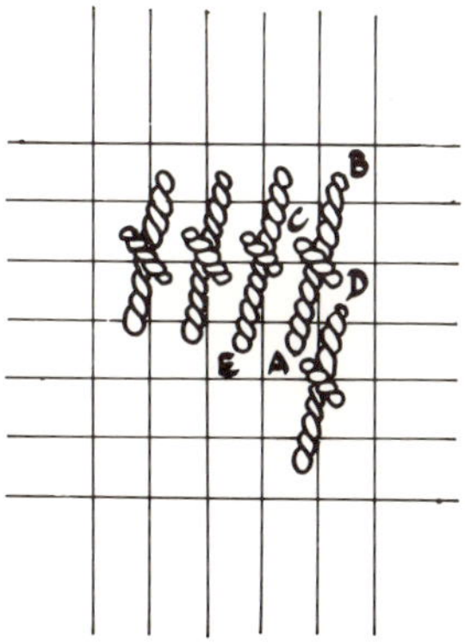

Fig. 2.72 Knitting stitch: the first row and beginning of the second row. Note how the stitches overlap.

times the wool is pulled through. The knotted stitch may be used for a background or filler.

1. Begin at A as shown in Fig. 2.72 and insert the needle at B, three threads above and one to the right. Bring the needle to the front at C, diagonally below and pull the wool to the front. To complete the stitch, insert the needle at D, diagonally below C, and bring it to the front at E, to the left of A, for the second stitch. Pull the wool through. Continue in the same manner to the end of the row and finish off.

2. Return to the right side of the canvas for the second row. Note that the stitches in the second and all subsequent rows overlap those in the preceeding row by one thread as shown in the illustration.

Upright Cross Stitch

The upright cross stitch is composed of a vertical stitch and a crossing horizontal stitch (photo 2.46). It may be used as a filler or a background stitch and is often a decorative addition to another stitch, for example, the triple leviathan stitch. It is quick to work and provides a durable backing. The upright cross does not distort and can be worked on either type canvas and in both directions, i.e. it is not necessary to turn the canvas as long as you make the crossings in the same direction. A very interesting effect is created when every other stitch is worked in a different colour.

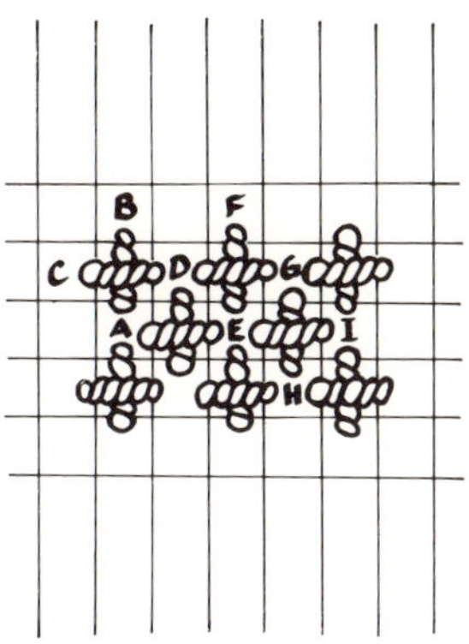

Fig. 2.73 Upright cross stitch. These three rows show how the crosses fit neatly together.

1. Come to the front at A as shown in Fig. 2.73 and make a vertical stitch to B, two threads above. Make the horizontal stitch by coming to the front at C, diagonally below and to the left of B, and inserting the needle at D, two threads to the right. Begin the second stitch by coming to the front at E, diagonally below and one to the right of D and repeat the vertical stitch by

Photo 2.46 Upright cross stitch.

inserting the needle at F, two threads above. Come to the front at D and make the horizontal stitch by inserting the needle at G, two threads to the right. Continue in this fashion to the end of the row.

2. The stitches in the second row fit between the stitches in the first row. To work the second row without turning the canvas, come to the front at H and make the vertical stitch by inserting the needle at G, two threads above. Come to the front at I, diagonally below and to the right, and insert the needle at E to complete the stitch. Continue in the same manner to the end of the row.

3. Work the odd rows as you did the first row and the even rows as you did the second.

Double Cross Stitch

A combination of a large cross stitch and an upright cross stitch, the double cross is quick to work. The backing is minimal and the stitch does not distort the canvas. It may be worked in one colour, but is particularly distinctive in two colours. Easily stitched on both single and penelope canvas, though most attractive on the latter, the double cross is an effective border or filler stitch provided you remember that it requires nine vertical and eight horizontal threads to complete the sequence (photo 2.47). Take special care in fitting the wool to the canvas or the stitch will lose its distinctiveness.

1. The first row is worked from left to right. Come up at A as shown in Fig. 2.74. Insert the needle at B, four threads diagonally above to the right. Come up at C, four threads to the left of B and make the second diagonal of the large cross to D, four threads below and to the right. Work the first upright cross coming to the front at E, two threads above and one to the left of

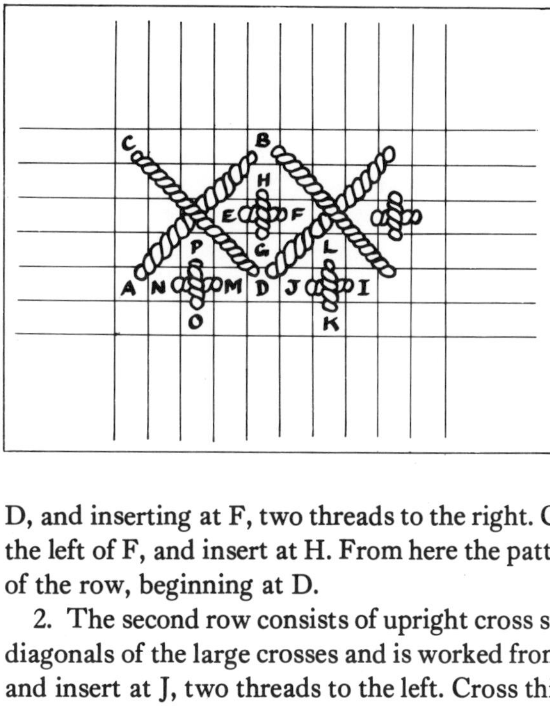

Photo 2.47 Double cross stitch.

Fig. 2.74 Double cross stitch. An easy stitch to work on both types of canvas.

D, and inserting at F, two threads to the right. Come up at G, diagonally to the left of F, and insert at H. From here the pattern repeats itself to the end of the row, beginning at D.

2. The second row consists of upright cross stitches worked between the diagonals of the large crosses and is worked from right to left. Come up at I and insert at J, two threads to the left. Cross this stitch by coming up at K and inserting at L, two threads above. Make the second upright cross by coming up at M, inserting at N, coming up at O and inserting at P. Continue to the end of the row.

3. The third and all subsequent odd rows are worked in the same manner as the first row and the fourth and all subsequent even rows are worked in the same manner as the second row.

Photo 2.48 Smyrna-cross stitch.

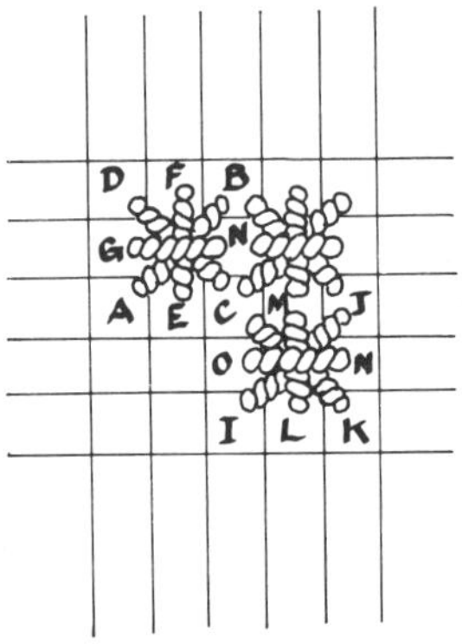

Fig. 2.75 Smyrna-cross stitch. A raised stitch that is excellent for decoration or emphasis.

Smyrna-cross Stitch

A combination of all three types of stitches, the Smyrna-cross stitch is an upright cross stitch worked on top of a cross stitch (photo 2.48). The result is interesting and is raised above the surface of the canvas. Because the same threads are covered more than once to complete the stitch, it is slow to work, but forms a padded backing. Worked in rows or singly, the Smyrna-cross stitch is excellent for both decoration and emphasis and is effective on either type of canvas. Similar to the upright cross, this stitch may be worked in both directions without having to turn the canvas. Take note that this stitch requires two horizontal and two vertical threads to complete a sequence.

1. Begin by working a cross stitch; come to the front at A as shown in Fig. 2.75. Insert the needle at B, two threads above and diagonally to the right. Return to the front at C, two threads directly below B. Complete the cross stitch by inserting the needle at D, two threads diagonally above and to the left. Work an upright cross stitch on top of this cross stitch by coming to the front at E, two threads below and one to the left of D and inserting the needle at F, two threads directly above. Complete the stitch by coming to the front at G, one thread below and to the left, and insert the needle at H, two threads to the right.
2. Begin the second stitch at C and continue to the end of the row.
3. To work the second row—in this instance, from right to left—begin the cross stitch at I in Fig. 2.75 and follow the same steps as previously, inserting the needle at J, returning to the front at K, and inserting the needle at C. Begin the upright cross at L and insert the needle at M, two threads above. However, the final horizontal stitch begins at N, one thread below and to the

Photo 2.49 Double leviathan stitch.

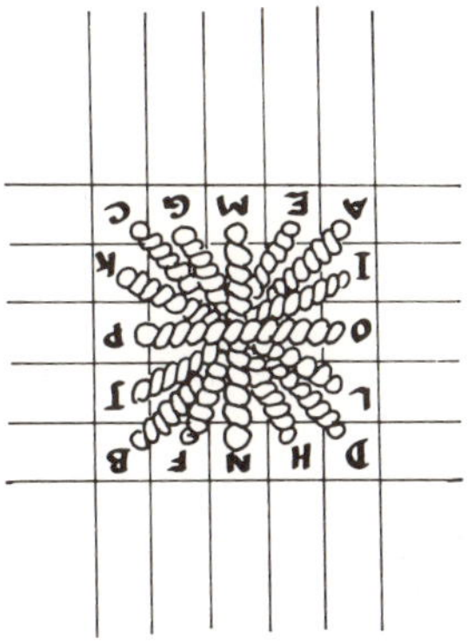

Fig. 2.76 Double leviathan stitch. Another raised stitch which is attractive but needs careful planning.

right of M, rather than to the left as in the previous row. Complete the stitch by inserting the needle at O.

4. Continue in the same manner to the end of the row, beginning the second stitch two threads to the left of I. Work all odd rows as you did the first row and all even rows as you did the second row.

Double Leviathan Stitch

A decorative stitch, the double leviathan is eight stitches of all three types worked over four threads (photo 2.49). Each individual stitch passes over the centre square and the double leviathan, like the Smyrna cross, has relief. The double leviathan provides only an average backing, but does not distort the canvas and may be worked on both types of canvas. It is important that the wool fits the canvas properly so that the stitch does not become too crowded and lose its distinctiveness. The double leviathan may be worked either in rows or individually and, if necessary, when working the stitch in rows, you can make one vertical stitch between the individual double leviathans. Remember to plan the spacing carefully when including this stitch in a design because it requires four horizontal and four vertical threads for completion.

1. Begin at A as shown in Fig. 2.76 and insert the needle at B, four threads diagonally above and to the right. Come to the front at C, four threads directly below. Insert the needle at D, four threads diagonally above and to the left, in line with A. Come to the front at E, four threads below and one to the right of D; insert the needle at F, two threads to the right and four above, beside B. Return to the front at G, four threads directly below, and insert the needle at H, two threads to the left and four above. Return to the front at I, one thread to the left and three below; insert the needle at J, four

threads to the right and two above. Return to the front at K, two threads directly below, and insert the needle at L, four threads to the left and two above. Return to the front at M, two threads to the right and three below, and make a vertical stitch to N, four threads above. Make the final stitch, a horizontal one, by returning to the front at O, two threads to the left and below, and insert the needle at P, four threads to the right.

2. Begin the second stitch at C and repeat the above instructions. Continue in this manner to the end of the row.

Triple Leviathan Stitch

The triple leviathan consists of twelve diagonal stitches that originate from the same hole and five decorative upright cross stitches (photo 2.50). It is unique in that it cannot be worked in rows and is used by itself as decoration or for emphasis. This stitch is best displayed on coarser canvas; it does not distort and is especially well-suited to multicolouring. The triple leviathan requires six vertical and six horizontal threads for completion.

1. Come to the front at A (Fig. 2.77); A should be at the centre of the space in which you are working the stitch. Insert the needle at B, two threads above and one to the right. Return to the front at A and insert at C, two threads above and two the right. Return to the front at A and insert the needle at D, one thread above and two to the right. Return to the front at A and insert the needle at E, one thread below and two to the right. Return to the front at A and insert the needle at F, two threads below and two to the right. Return to the front at A and insert the needle at G, two threads below and one to the right. Repeat this pattern on the left half of the stitch, returning to the front each time at A and inserting the needle at H, I, J, K, L, and M. If you are using a second colour for the upright cross stiches, finish off at this point; otherwise, you can continue with the same piece of wool.

2. Work the five upright cross stitches as shown in Fig. 2.78, coming up at N and inserting the needle at O. Return to the surface at M and insert the needle at B. Come to the front at D and insert the needle at E. Return to the front at P and insert the needle at Q. The third upright cross begins at R; insert the needle at S and return to the front at G; insert the needle at H. To work the fourth upright cross, come to the front at J and insert the needle at K; return to the front at T and insert the needle at U. Make the final upright cross (not shown in Fig. 2.78) by coming to the front at S, inserting the needle at N, returning to the front at U and inserting the needle at P. Finish off.

Leaf Stitch

The leaf stitch consists of ten slanting stitches and one vertical worked in the pattern of a leaf (photo 2.51). The individual stitches cover three and four threads, so they are somewhat prone to snagging. The backing is well

Photo 2.50 Triple leviathan stitch.

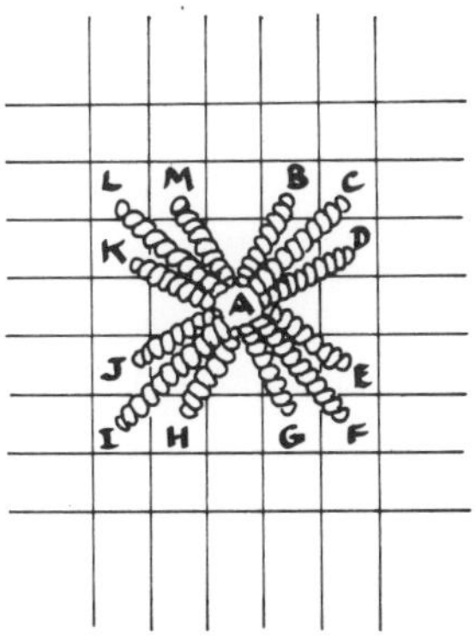

Fig. 2.77 Triple leviathan stitch: the basic twelve diagonal stitches.

Fig. 2.78 The completed triple leviathan stitch.

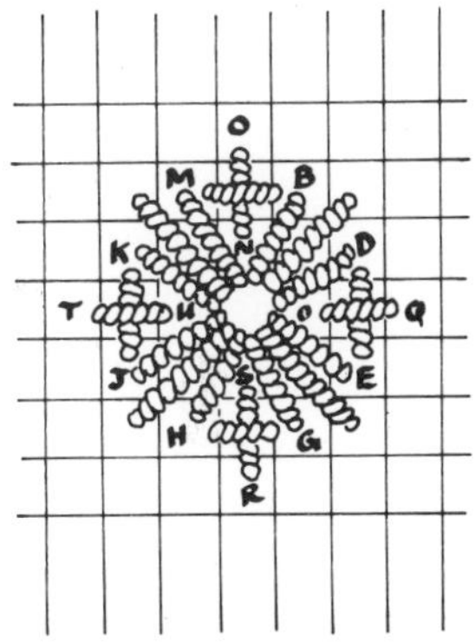

Photo 2.51 Leaf stitch.

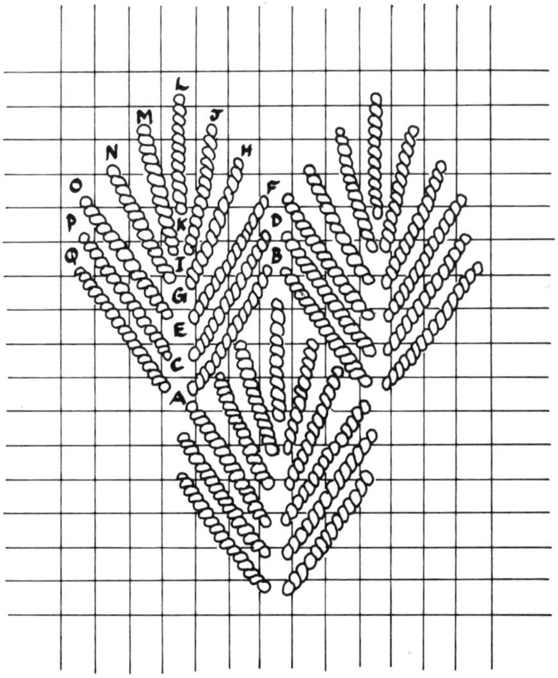

Fig. 2.79 The leaf-like pattern of this stitch makes a very attractive background.

padded and the stitch is quick to work. Best when worked on single canvas, the leaf stitch makes a delightful background, border, filler or accent stitch and it does not distort the canvas. When planning to include this stitch in a design, you should remember that one full stitch sequence requires nine horizontal and six vertical threads.

1. Come up at A as shown in Fig. 2.79 and insert the needle at B, three threads to the right and four threads above. Return to the front at C, one thread above A, and insert the needle at D, one thread above B. Come up at E, one thread above C, and insert the needle at F, one thread above D. Return to the front at G and insert the needle at H, two threads to the right and four threads above. Return to the front at I, one thread above G, and insert the needle at J, one thread to the right and four above. Make the vertical stitch next by coming to the front at K and inserting the needle at L, four threads above. Come to the front at I, one thread below K and insert the needle at M, four threads diagonally above and in line with J. Come up at G and insert the needle at N, two threads to the left and four above, in line with H. Return to the front at E and insert the needle at O, three threads to the left and four above, in line with F. Come up at C and insert the needle at P, one thread below O. Come up at A and insert the needle at Q, one thread below P. You can also work this stitch starting from the left side and progressing around to the right side of the leaf.

Note: From the illustration, you can see how the stitches fit beside one another if they are worked as a background. To make the edges flush, fill in

Photo 2.52 *Stem stitch.*

with part of a leaf. You can make the whole smaller by leaving out the bottom pair of stitches.

Stem Stitch

The stem stitch consists of pairs of diagonal stitches with short vertical stitches worked between them (photo 2.52). It is an attractive stitch that can be worked on both types of canvas. The backing is durable and the stitch does not distort the canvas. It is quick to work and may be used as filler or as a decorative border. It is especially appealing when the diagonal and vertical stitches are worked in different colours. When using this stitch in a design, remember that each row needs four vertical threads.

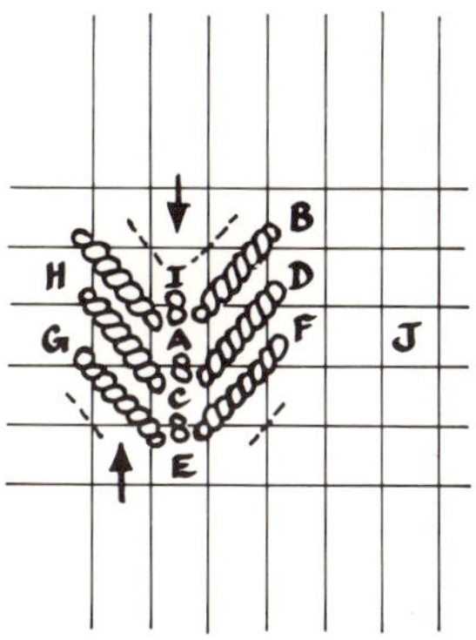

Fig. 2.80 Stem stitch: a durable stitch that can be worked on both types of canvas.

1. The first row of diagonal stitches is worked from the top to the bottom of the canvas. Come up at A (see Fig. 2.80) and insert the needle at B, two threads above and two to the right. Return to the front at C, one thread below A and make the second stitch to D, one thread below B. Come up at E and insert the needle at F. Continue to the end of the row.
2. The second row of diagonals is worked from the bottom to the top of the canvas. Come up at G, in line with F and insert the needle at E. Come up at H, one thread above G and insert the needle at C. Continue to the end of the row.
3. To make the vertical stitches, come up at I, down at A; up at C, down at A; up at E, down at C.
4. Finish off the row and begin the next row at J.

Note: Fill in the bare canvas with tent stitches worked in the appropriate directions as indicated in the illustration.

Photo 2.53 Diamond eyelet stitch.

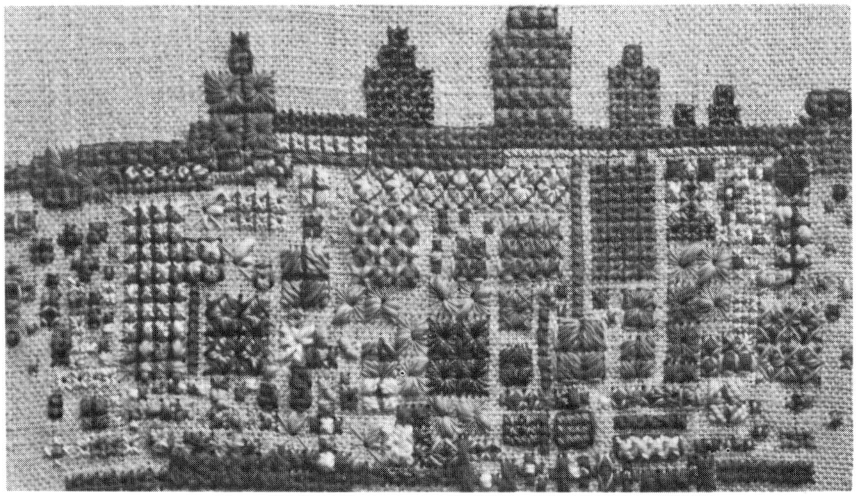

Photo 2.54 Stitched on yellow linen, this piece explores the technique of leaving part of the background bare. Through the use of different textures of wool and cotton, the designer has created a startling effect with a small number of stitches, especially the diamond eyelet stitch. Designed and stitched by Jean M. F. Carter.

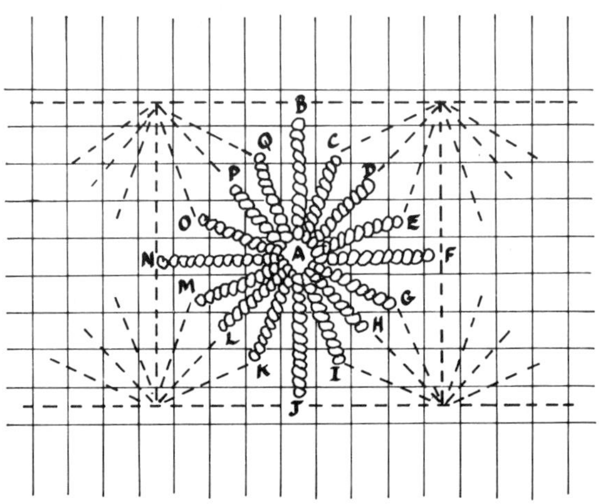

Fig. 2.81 Diamond eyelet stitch is slow to work but is excellent for emphasis.

Diamond Eyelet Stitch

The diamond eyelet stitch (photo 2.53) is a combination of diagonal, vertical and horizontal stitches, all radiating out from one point; the wool must fit the canvas exactly or bare canvas will show around the edges. The very interesting pattern of this stitch is fairly slow to work, but the backing is well padded and firm. Best worked on single canvas, it makes an unusual background if you are prepared to spend the time stitching it; otherwise use it as a filler or for emphasis (photo 2.54). Note that the stitch requires eight vertical and horizontal threads to complete a sequence.

1. Come up at A as shown in Fig. 2.81 and insert the needle at B, four threads above. Return to A and insert the needle at C, three threads above and one to the right. Continue to follow the letters through the alphabet to Q, each time coming up at A.

Note: Photo 2.53 will show you how the stitches fit together. To cover the bare threads, fill in with as much of the stitch sequence as possible, as shown by the dotted lines in the drawing.

Triangle Stitch

Consisting of four triangles, with a cross stitch in each corner to form a square, the triangle stitch is a unique filler (photo 2.55). It can be worked rapidly, but is prone to snagging. The backing is well padded rather than firm and the stitch is best worked on single canvas; it does not distort. Ten vertical and horizontal threads are required to complete a sequence; remember this when including it in your design.

1. Come up at A as shown in Fig. 2.82 and insert the needle at B, two threads below. Return to the front at C, one thread to the right of A, and

Photo 2.55 Triangle stitch.

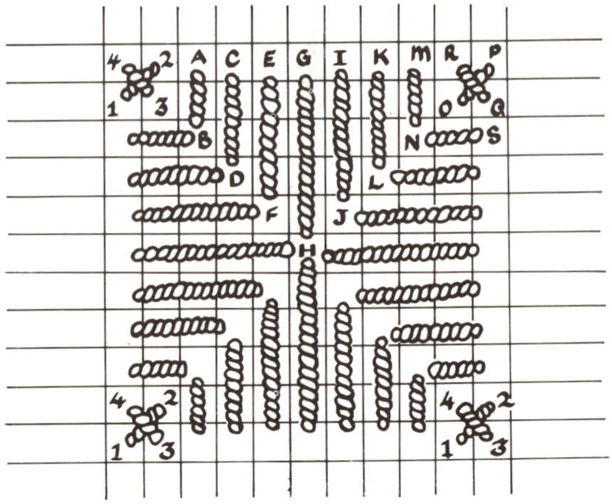

Fig. 2.82 Triangle stitch. This can be worked rapidly and is a unique filler.

insert the needle at D, three threads below. Come up at E, beside C, and insert at F, four threads below. Come to the front at G, beside E, and insert at H, five threads below. Come up at I, beside G, and insert at J, four threads below. Come up at K, beside I, and insert at L, three threads below. Come up at M, beside K, and insert at N, two threads below. Make the cross stitch by coming up at O and inserting at P, and then coming up at Q and insert at R. From here the pattern repeats.

2. The next stitch sequence is worked horizontally. Begin at S and insert the needle at N and so on. Remember to work each cross stitch in the same manner as the first cross; the numbers in Fig. 2.82 indicate the steps when working each cross.

3. The third sequence is stitched vertically, the fourth is stitched horizontally.

Looped Stitches

Looped stitches are worked either by winding the wool around the needle or by making a loop of wool that sticks out from the surface of the canvas. The two presented here are raised from the surface of the canvas, and thus have a texture; they can be used very effectively for emphasis or as fillers.

Turkey Tufting Stitch

Turkey tufting (photo 2.56) makes a pile similar to that of a shag rug. It can be cut or looped, depending upon your design. The length of the pile is adjustable as well; the longer the pile, the more wool the stitch consumes. Turkey tufting can be worked on both single and penelope canvas and does not distort. It is quick to work, and can be used for an entire design, small prominent areas or as a fringe. It is perfect for animal fur or anything else you want to be fuzzy. This stitch must be worked from left to right only and is stitched in every other horizontal row. On finishing each row, you must

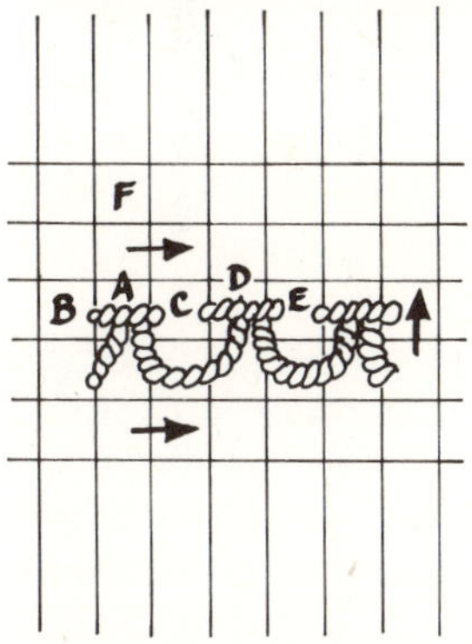

Photo 2.56 Turkey tufting stitch.

Fig. 2.83 Turkey tufting makes a pile and is a very versatile stitch. It can be used for emphasis, for a prominent area or as a fringe.

finish off and return to the left side of the canvas. To prevent the stitches tangling, work the rows from the bottom to the top of the canvas.

1. Start at the front of the canvas and insert your needle at A as shown in Fig. 2.83. Let the end of the wool hang free on the front of the canvas to the length you want your finished pile to be. Hold the end in place with your left thumb and come to the front at B, beside A. Make the next stitch by inserting the needle at C, two threads to the right of B. Return to the front at A. Pull the wool fairly tight.

2. Begin the second stitch by inserting the needle at D, two threads to the right of A, holding a loop of wool the length of the first end in place with your thumb. Come to the front at C. Insert the needle at E, two threads to the right and return to the front at D. Continue to the end of the row. Finish off by cutting the wool, so that the last piece hangs free.

3. To work the second row, return to the left side of the canvas and begin the row at F. If you wish, you can clip the loops of the stitches, depending upon your own personal preference and the design.

Twisted Knot Stitch

The twisted knot (photo 2.57) is adapted from the French knot of embroidery. It gives a very interesting effect to canvas embroidery when used as a filler or accent stitch. Traditionally, the stitch has been used as flower centres with great success and it is most effective worked as an individual stitch, in clusters rather than in rows. The stitch does not distort the canvas, gives minimal backing and may be worked on both types of canvas.

1. Come up at A as shown in Fig. 2.84. Form a loop and hold it in place with your left thumb as shown, then slide the needle into the loop.
2. Turn the needle clockwise, as indicated by the dotted line in Fig. 2.85, twisting the wool around the needle.
3. Still holding the loop tightly, insert the needle at B, diagonally above and to the left of A, as shown in Fig. 2.86. Be especially careful that the wool is kept taut between A and B. Gently draw the wool to the back of the canvas, controlling it with your left thumb. Do not pull the wool too tight or bare canvas will show. At the same time, try to keep the tension even because this will regulate the size of your knots.

Note: To increase the size of the knots add an extra strand of wool. The position of B can be on any of the four diagonals from A, which ever you find most convenient.

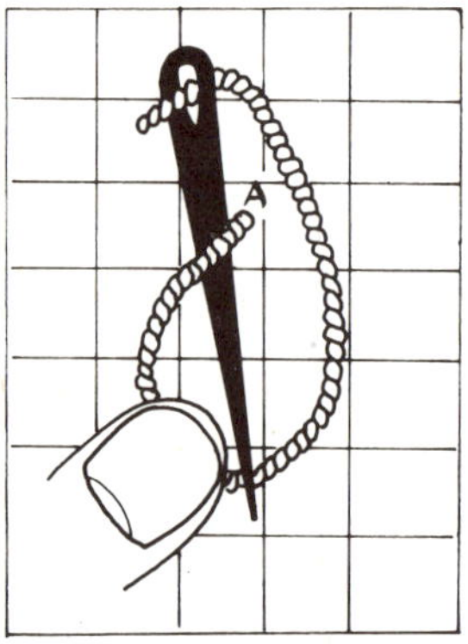

Fig. 2.84 Twisted knot stitch. First stage: making the loop.

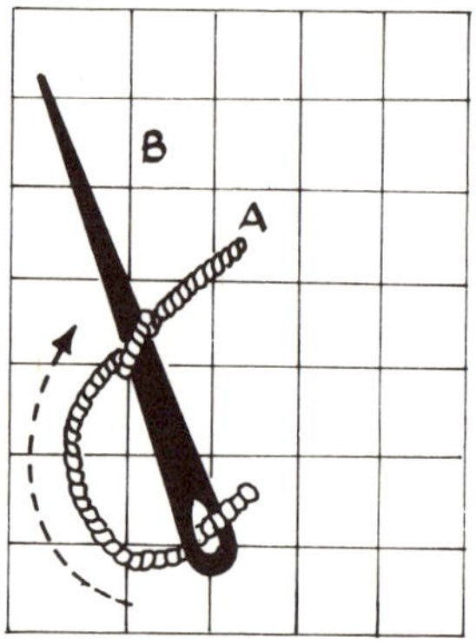

Fig. 2.85 Twisted knot stitch. Second stage: twisting the needle in the loop.

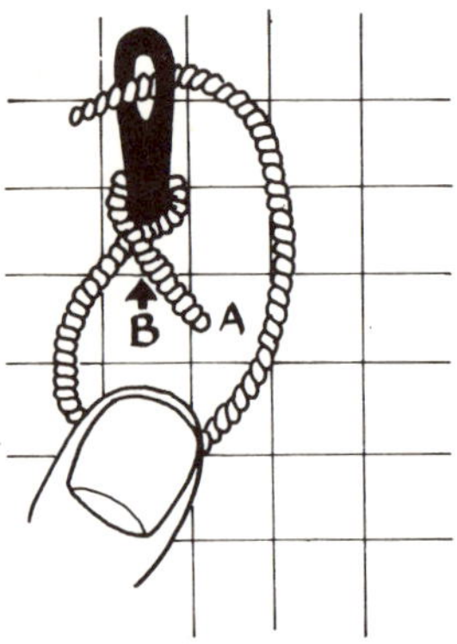

Fig. 2.86 Twisted knot stitch. Third stage: inserting the needle at B to complete the stitch.

Photo 2.57 Twisted knot stitch.

3 Stitching a sampler

A sampler, more than any other stitchery project, embodies the historical tradition of canvas embroidery. Originally called Sam cloths, samplers came into use during the sixteenth century when needlework was at a peak of popularity and professionalism. The earliest dated sampler that has survived is one stitched in 1598. Throughout the sixteenth century, samplers filled the need for a permanent record of patterns and stitches because the price of the scarce pattern books was prohibitive. Families preserved their cherished samplers, to which the stitcher added as his or her knowledge grew. With the increased availability of pattern books during the next two centuries, the sampler continued in popularity and became the proof of the needlework skill of every young woman. No seventeenth- or eighteenth-century woman's education was complete until she had stitched 'in silks and gold thread a Sampler with a bordering of Drawn Work, and a centre filled with representations of animals, flowers, and trees, accompanied by verses appropriate to the undertaking' (p. 433, Volume II, *Encyclopedia of Victorian Needlework*, S. F. A. Caulifield, Dover Publications, New York, U.S.A., 1972).

In addition to being a permanent record, today's sampler is used as the first practice-ground for stitches. There is no better method of learning canvas embroidery stitches than to work a number of individual stitches repeatedly so that they become firmly fixed in your memory; for this purpose, the sampler is the perfect medium. Stitching a sampler helps you to get the feeling of the wool on the canvas and to develop a consistent tension; as explained in Chapter 2, pulling the yarn too tight allows bare canvas to show through and will mar the smooth texture of your canvas. You will also have an opportunity to see how the different stitches look next to one another.

Photo 3.1 These two Victorian samplers show the use of a sampler as a record of both stitches and design. (Courtesy of the Embroiderers' Guild, London)

Photo 3.2 This sampler is from the collection at the Victoria & Albert Museum. (Crown copyright, Victoria & Albert Museum, London)

Photo 3.3 This design is visually pleasing as well as being an exercise in the positioning and the execution of stitches. Designed and worked by Miss N. Dowling.

A sampler gives you greater freedom than a more formal project. You need not be inhibited as to choice of colour, size or shape, because you will want to preserve your sampler for your own use and reference rather than to give it away. You do not have to consider the colour of the sofa on which a pillow will find its home or the room in which an embroidered chair will sit. In fact, the more colour, the better. This is also an excellent opportunity to experiment with stitches that lend themselves to multicolouring.

Your sampler may take any number of shapes and sizes. It could be square, circular (although this is a rather complicated shape for a beginner), rectangular or the traditional seventeenth-century long and narrow piece of canvas, worked from top to bottom and added to over the years. If you decide to make a sampler that will have a practical use, rather than a sampler for the sake of being a sampler, this will obviously influence the shape and dimensions in a different manner. A square sampler could be made into a pillow, a rectangular one into a carrier or a sewing bag, and any shape at all can be hung on the wall. Take care not to make the sampler so large that it becomes a disheartening task; it should be an adventure in learning and a creative spark for future projects. If the first canvas takes an inordinately long time to stitch, beginners tend to become discouraged and may not finish the piece; worse still, they may never stitch another canvas again. So, be honest with yourself in selecting the dimensions of your sampler, and make the canvas only as big as your enthusiasm.

Having made the selection of colour, shape and dimensions, you are ready to choose the design. Try to keep the pattern simple because this requires the least amount of planning and lets you concentrate on the stitches themselves. You might want to do something as basic as working two or three rows of selected stitches horizontally or vertically across the canvas, giving a striped effect, or you could be more traditional and work two columns of squares, each in a different stitch. Filling a rectangle or a square with multi-shaped patches of individual stitches is another idea (see photo 3.3). This design is more complicated because you will have to be certain that you have the correct number of threads in the squares where you plan to work those more elaborate stitches that require an exact number of threads. Otherwise, you might try grouping together one stitch from each of the seven categories, or all those in one category, in individual sections of the sampler, or just experimenting at random with any stitch you like. A challenging and traditional plan is to work all the letters of the alphabet, both upper and lower cases, and the numbers from one to ten in different stitches. Surround the letters and numbers with a border of one or two rows of stitches and fill in the background. As a final suggestion, you could copy the pattern of an antique sampler from a needlework book. In the last two instances, you may have to apply the design to the canvas or use a graph-paper guide to assist you in stitching.

All that remains to be done is to purchase the materials and prepare the canvas. You will need between a half and a full yard of canvas (depending upon the size of your sampler), yarn, a tapestry needle, a roll of 1-in. wide masking tape or a packet of fabric binding (to prevent the edges of the canvas from unravelling), and a waterproof, felt-tipped pen (to mark the outer edges of your piece). If you have chosen a design that requires painting, you will also need some coloured, waterproof, felt-tipped markers of acrylic paint.

Detailed instructions for preparing and painting the canvas appear in Chapter 4; these directions should be consulted if this is your first piece. Briefly, cut the canvas to the proper size, mark the borders of the stitched piece with the waterproof felt-tipped pen, bind the edges with masking tape or fabric binding, and paint the canvas. Before cutting the canvas, add three extra rows on each side for seam allowance and a further 2 inches of bare canvas beyond that. For example, if your canvas is going to be 4 × 12 in. when finished, cut the canvas $8\frac{1}{2} \times 16\frac{1}{2}$ in.—assuming the three rows of seam allowance to equal approximately $\frac{1}{4}$ in.; $4\frac{1}{2} \times 12\frac{1}{2}$ in. to be stitched plus the 2-inch border of bare canvas on all sides.

One of the major reasons that I have recommended a sampler as your first project is that it provides an opportunity to practise all the stitches that you will use in other pieces. Remember that with a sampler, the emphasis is on the stitches rather than on the design. Certainly a sophisticated design is a welcome change, but concentrate upon the stitches and the way they are worked (photo 3.4). Use an average-sized canvas that displays the details of each stitch to a better advantage than fine canvas. When your sampler is completed, you will have given yourself both a thorough lesson in canvas embroidery stitches and a physical record of every stitch you have worked.

Photo 3.4 Another design suggestion for a sampler.

4 Designs and applying them to canvas

If, as you read the title of this chapter, you thought to yourself, 'I can't draw a design', please try to suppress that preconception. Design is a word with a wide range of meanings and canvas-embroidery designing is no exception; colour selection and the arrangement of stitches are just as important to a design as the subject. You can always copy and enlarge or reduce someone else's art work, but the choice of stitches and colouring is always entirely your own. And it is the stitches and colours that give texture and life to a design.

Don't be afraid to try a sketch—you can throw it away if you don't like it; besides, it may well be very good. If you feel more comfortable at first by interpreting someone else's drawing, do that; practice in copying and interpreting other people's work helps you to get the feel of sketching and the rhythm in your wrist and fingers. Gradually you can develop the confidence and the ability to create a design of your own. So, don't be afraid and don't be embarrassed . . . and don't be limited by convention!

With the onset of the most recent wave of popularity of canvas embroidery has come a new freedom in the choice of subjects and in styles of designing. Not every canvas looks like a fine-line drawing; many have become more casual, under the influence of a less formal way of living. Most assuredly, there are designers who continue to produce traditional subjects, but modern designs of commonplace subjects are becoming increasingly popular. Cartoon and book characters are reproduced on canvas too—witness the canvases of Beatrix Potter and Walt Disney characters. With the help of mass-produced kits, needlework shops have contributed to the popularity of canvas embroidery and have facilitated the purchasing of the basic materials needed for the craft. As canvas embroidery becomes more widely practised, and the materials more readily available, so more people are creating their own designs. This trend can only encourage those people who have yet to try their hand at designing.

Choosing your design: Inspiration

If you have any trouble finding inspiration for your first design, there are many places and publications which can help you. As I have already mentioned, other works of art—recognized or not—are a start and magazines, books and needlework leaflets are reliable and easily accessible sources. Make a visit to a museum and search the bookshop for an idea. Fabric and your own clothing could produce a favourite motif for a repeated-pattern design and wrapping paper, greetings cards, and art postcards are further sources for similar attractive motifs. Children's colouring books are usually full of animated animals, flowers, and other subjects that can be adapted to your own taste with a bit of imagination. Scan the encyclopedia, and floral and horticultural guidebooks or magazines, save your pictorial calendars and visit your local decorating shop to browse through the wallpaper books.

The important thing to remember when you are composing your design is that it will be stitched on a squared canvas. This 'squareness' will influence the appearance of some shapes when stitched. Straight lines, diagonals leaning to the right, and square and rectangular shapes whose edges are *parallel* with the warp and woof (vertical and horizontal) threads of the canvas will retain their true shape when they are stitched. However, some curving shapes, all diagonal lines leaning to the left, and all circular, rectangular, and square shapes placed *on the diagonal* will have zigzag edges when they are stitched. There is no way to avoid this, so don't be alarmed when your diagonal lines leaning to the left aren't perfect—they're supposed to be that way. In any case, except on very large-holed canvas, the zigzag is not particularly marked and the eye smooths the edges naturally. To attain the neatest and most uniform line when stitching these diagonal lines and shapes, work your stitches in step-like progression (Fig. 4.1).

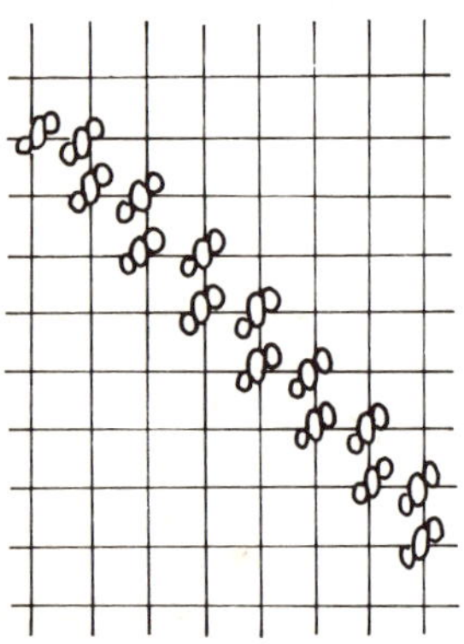

Fig. 4.1 Work your stitches in step-like progression to attain a neat line when stitching diagonal lines and shapes.

Large stylized forms and patterns can be more successfully adapted to canvas than can small, detailed shapes and can be stitched on an average sized canvas very easily. However, if you want to introduce detail into your design, you should use a finer-meshed canvas. You will remember that these canvases accommodate more stitches per inch and consequently lend themselves to more intricate patterns. Always consider the sizes of canvas meshes when you are composing a design.

Choice of Stitches

After you have chosen your design and colours, you are ready to decide which stitches to use and where. In the beginning, until you become well acquainted with the stitches, the safe approach is to maintain a balance between the basic stitches and the more elaborate ones. Try using the latter as highlights or in the background of your design. Remember that the basic

Photo 4.1 This familiar Beatrix Potter character was stitched by J. Stevens.

Photo 4.2A and B Designed and stitched by Moyra McNeill, these motifs could be elaborated into a repeated-motif design. (Courtesy of the Embroiderers' Guild)

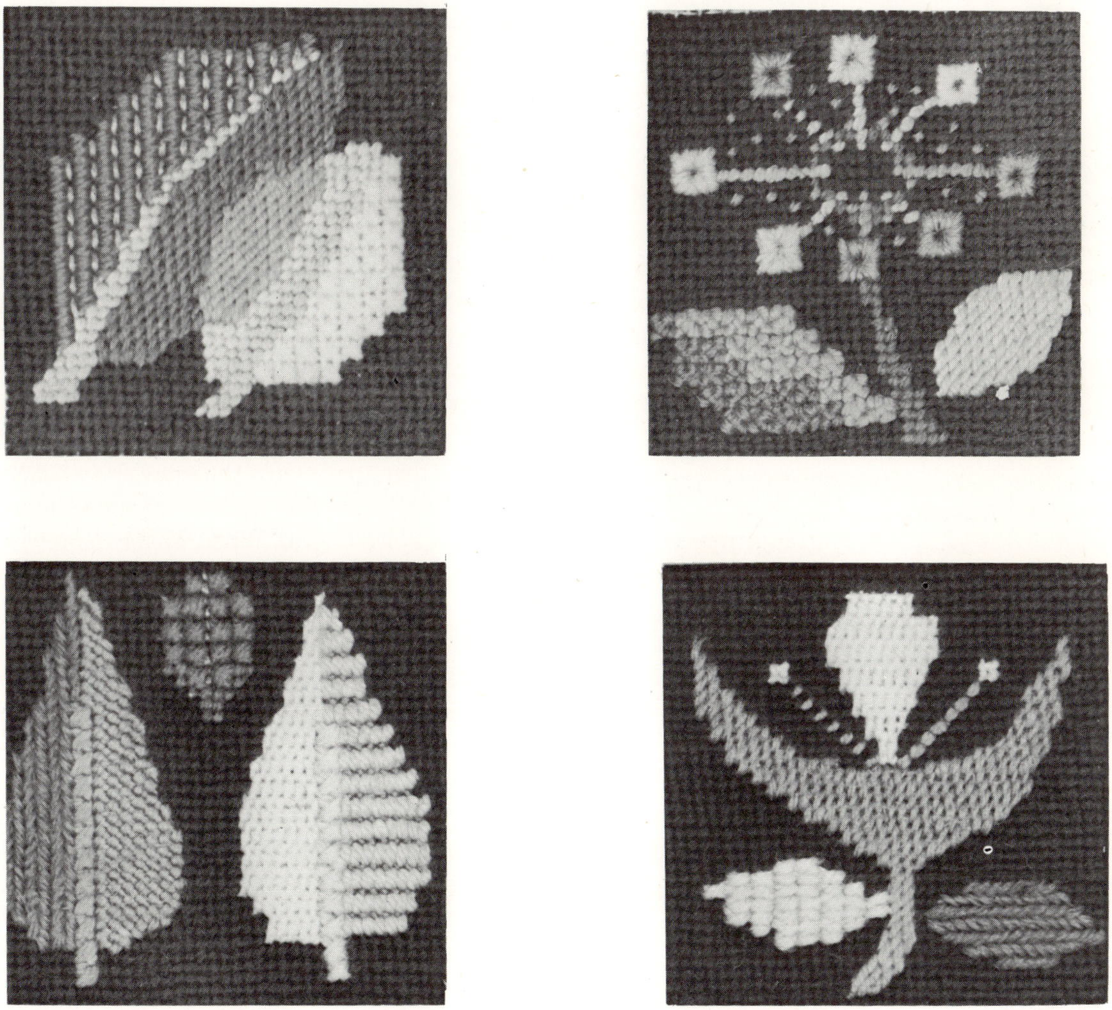

Photo 4.3 This design was copied from one in a collection of pieces at the Victoria & Albert Museum. Stitched by Dr Wood.

Photo 4.4 This piece, Colour Sequence 2, *beautifully illustrates the delicate shading that can be achieved in canvas embroidery. Designed and stitched by Joanne Graham.*

stitches are excellent for detailed shaded designs, and that the fancier stitches can be beautifully displayed in simple, bold designs. Excessive use of the fancy stitches in your canvas can result in a hodge-podge of activity which almost obliterates the essence of your design.

'Combination' designs

Often you will find a design that you can faithfully reproduce on canvas; however, just as frequently, you will discover from various sources a number of potential design components that you would like to combine into one composition. You can do this with ease by first marking the dimensions of your design on a blank piece of paper. Next, trace each of the components on separate pieces of tracing paper that are roughly the same size as each of the subjects. Lay them on the blank paper and experiment with different arrangements until you find one that pleases you. When you are happy with your composition, copy the entire arrangement on to another piece of tracing paper, colour the design, and transfer it to the canvas.

Sizing the Design

When you have a design with the wrong dimensions, the 'squares method' is a convenient way to enlarge or reduce it. You will need a ruler, a sheet of drawing paper and a pencil. Whether you are enlarging or reducing a design, the principle is the same. Divide your design into squares of equal size (if the design is drawn or printed on something on which you cannot or do not want to write, trace the design on to another piece of paper before squaring it off). Mark the desired dimensions on a piece of drawing paper and divide this shape into the same number of squares as you ruled on your design. Obviously, the dimensions of the squares will differ, but the impor-

Photo 4.5 This Hungarian stitch piece was worked during the eighteenth century. Hungarian is another name for the Bargello or Florentine stitch. (Crown copyright, Victoria & Albert Museum)

tant point is to have the same number on both the design and the drawing paper. (If you are enlarging your design, the squares of the project will be larger than those of your design; if you are reducing your design, the squares of the project will be smaller than those of the design.) In each square of the drawing paper sketch the contents of the corresponding square in the design (see Fig. 4.2).

Preparing the Canvas

When the design is completed, you should then turn your attention to preparing the canvas itself. Regardless of the dimensions of your canvas and the size of the meshes, you can treat all canvas the same way during the preliminary stages, i.e. cut the canvas to the proper size, bind the edges, and outline the dimensions of your project. But, before you cut any canvas, you must make three accurate measurements: the first and most obvious is the dimensions of the design, the secind is a finishing allowance, and the third is a border of unstitched canvas.

After you have established the dimensions of the design, you must add

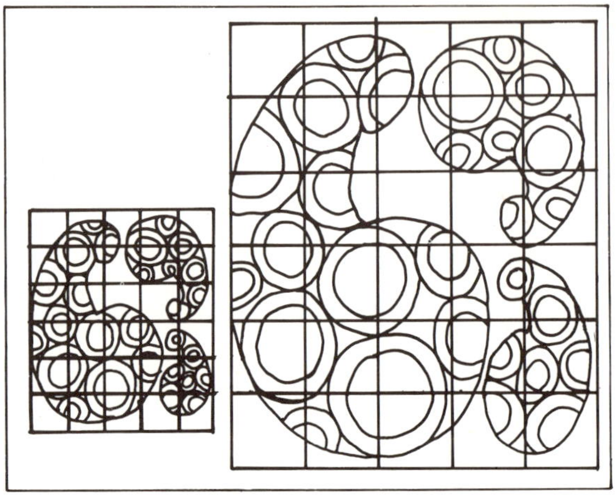

Fig. 4.2 Transferring a design: the 'squares method'.

some extra rows to each of the four sides of the piece as a finishing allowance. This allowance is not separate from the design, but is an extension of it, and is stitched in the same manner. The amount of finishing allowance will vary depending upon the nature of your project. If you are making something to be sewn together, add three extra rows to each side for seam allowance. If your project is to be mounted, the number of additional rows depends upon the mesh size of your canvas and the thickness of the mounting board; an average allowance is two rows, but add more rows if your piece is to be stitched on fine canvas. This stitched finishing allowance should be slightly wider than the thickness of the mounting board so that there are enough stitched rows to tack to the back of the mounting board.

The border of unstitched canvas is added beyond the finishing allowance, and will be used during blocking (see Chapter 5). Allow 2 inches of bare canvas on each of the four sides. For example, if you are making a pillow that is designed to be 12 × 16 in. when completed, you should first add the three extra rows for seams, increasing the size of the stitched canvas to approximately 12½ × 16½ in. (Seam allowance of coarser canvases will be larger because the rows are wider: this measurement is based upon 10 to the inch canvas.) Next, add the 2-inch border of plain canvas, increasing the entire canvas size to 16½ × 20½ in. This is the size you will cut.

After you have calculated the appropriate size for the canvas (including the 2-inch border), make a mark with the waterproof, felt-tipped pen where each corner will be. It is imperative that the pen is waterproof; if not, it could run on to the wool when the stitched canvas is being block and ruin your piece. So make certain that you buy the right type of pen and to be doubly sure, check the waterproofness yourself by making a mark with the pen on a small piece of canvas and putting it in a glass of water overnight. If the water is discoloured in the morning, you will know you can't use that pen on your canvas, whatever the manufacturer may claim about the product.

Take a sturdy pair of scissors and cut the canvas between the meshes

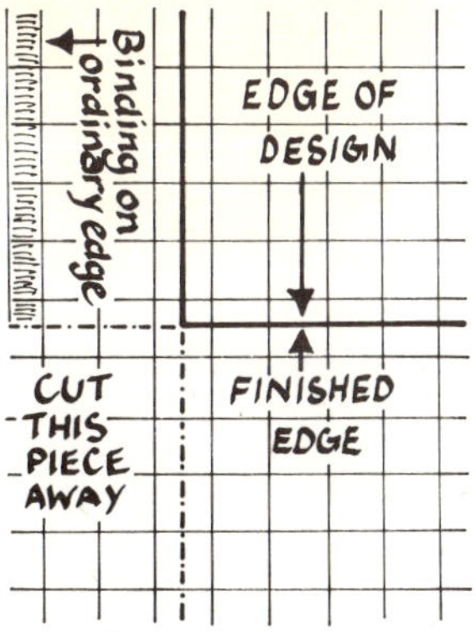

Fig. 4.3 Preparing a finished edge.

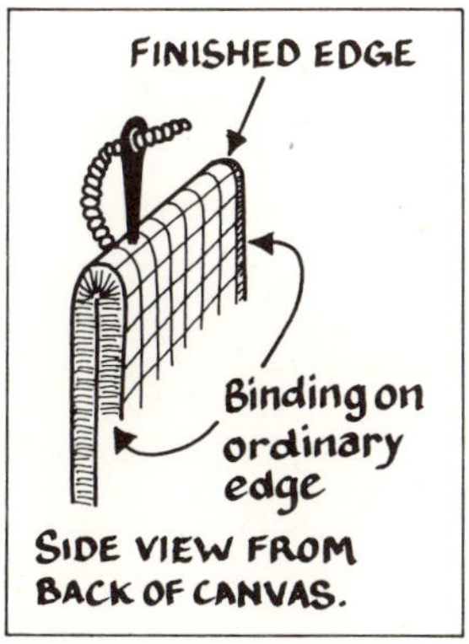

Fig. 4.4 Preparing a finished edge on penelope canvas.

(intersections of the threads). Any selvage should run along a vertical edge. Mark the dimensions, including both the design and the finishing allowance, on the canvas with the waterproof felt-tipped pen. (You may find it easier to draw the dimensions on the canvas before you cut it; this is entirely up to you. I prefer the first method because working with a large uncut piece of canvas is rather unwieldly.) Always cut the canvas in a square or rectangle, even if you are stitching a circular design.

To prevent the cut canvas from unravelling, you must bind the edges. One of the numerous ways of doing this is to double over the edges of the canvas twice and stitch the 'hem' in place with strong cotton thread. Alternatively, there are three types of tape you can use: iron-on tape, fabric-binding tape or masking tape. Whichever one you use, the principle is the same: fold the tape over the raw edge of the canvas, $\frac{1}{2}$ inch on each side, and either machine-stitch (with the fabric-binding tape) or iron (with the iron-on tape) it in place. In the case of masking tape, run the handle of your scissors along the taped edges of both the front and the back of the canvas, applying considerable pressure, until the weave of the canvas makes an impression on the tape. This is to ensure that the tape stays in place while you stitch your canvas.

Before continuing with the next step, you may be interested to learn how to prepare the canvas when stitching a project, such as a Christmas stocking or a pocket, with a finished edge. Briefly, this involves folding the canvas over and stitching through both layers as if they were a single thickness. Two finished edges are the most that any project should have, and these should be opposite each other rather than adjacent because more than two thicknesses of canvas become bulky and difficult to stitch. More important, you should not put tacks or pins into a finished edge because they will leave marks and you will therefore have a problem in blocking your piece (see Chapter 5). Keeping blocking in mind, it is advisable to use stitches that distort the canvas to a minimum. In general, vertical stitches cause less distortion than diagonal stitches; of the three ways to work the basic diagonal stitch, the basket-weave distorts the canvas least.

To prepare the finished edge, cut the canvas on the proposed side five rows wider than the design. This edge will not have the usual 2 inches of bare canvas around the design, whereas the three (or two) others will be treated normally. To prevent bulky corners, cut the canvas as indicated in Fig. 4.3. Put a thin line of all-purpose white glue along the cut edges and let it dry. Making certain that there are two rows of threads along the edge, turn the excess canvas to the back of the piece. If you are stitching single canvas, there will be two rows of canvas; when using penelope canvas with its double threads, a single row is sufficient. Align the meshes of the two layers of canvas and stitch through both thicknesses—including the edge—as if it were one (see Fig. 4.4). If you prefer, you may baste the folded over piece of canvas in place.

Using a Graph-paper Guide

Once you have marked the dimensions, cut the canvas and bound the edges, you must weigh the advantages and disadvantages of applying the design to the canvas. *Transferring* the design to the canvas is simply a matter of tracing on the design. However, if you use a graph-paper guide, you do not transfer the design at all, but stitch on a blank canvas; the position of each stitch is indicated on the graph paper and you must continually refer to it as you work your pattern. The advantage of this method is that you can see exactly how your stitched design will look on the canvas without actually doing the stitching—even down to the zigzag diagonal lines. However, the disadvantage of having constantly to refer to a paper guide before making each and every stitch outweights its merits. Part of the creativity involved in doing canvas embroidery is deciding how to fit the stitches into and around the shapes; a graph-paper guide takes away some of this challenge and spontaneity and adds unnecessary tedium. Furthermore, a canvas with a transferred design is much more convenient—you don't have to worry about having your paper guide with you when you take your canvas away from home. This enables you to pick up stitching wherever you stopped with a maximum of ease, and gives you the freedom to stitch any section of the canvas rather than having to follow a rigid pathway from the centre of the canvas to the edges.

After these somewhat biased remarks, if you still want to stitch with a graph-paper guide, it is an easy task. The least complicated method is to buy graph paper with the same number of squares per inch as your canvas has meshes per inch. Failing that, you can divide the canvas and the graph paper into equivalent squares; 1-inch squares are a workable size.

Rule the dimensions of your design on the graph paper and divide it vertically and horizontally through the centre. Sketch or trace the design on to the graph paper. (To trace on to graph paper, tape your design to a window and tape the graph paper over the design, so that the natural light shining through both pieces of paper makes the graph paper transparent.) Block in the shapes of the design, square by square, following the lines of the design as closely as possible as shown in Fig. 4.5. Divide the graph paper into 1-inch squares (you can buy graph paper that is already marked with dark lines every inch and save yourself this part of the task). Find the centre of the canvas by folding it into quarters and mark it with the waterproof felt-tipped pen or a pin. Divide the canvas into 1-inch squares and mark them. Begin stitching in the middle of the design and work towards the edges.

Applying the Design to the Canvas

If, however, you have chosen to apply the design to the canvas, find a working surface that is slightly larger than your intended project. You will need to stick tacks into it, so be sure it is a surface suitable for this purpose; I use a piece of chipboard that is both inexpensive and not too hard for tacks. Lay your design on the working surface and place the canvas on top of the design. Secure the design and the canvas to the working surface by taping them or tacking them with map pins (also called push pins). The best type, with a head about $\frac{3}{8}$ in. long, is easy to pull out of the board; they are available in most stationers and art supply stores. If you use map pins, start by tacking opposite corners, pulling the canvas into place if necessary; then put the pins around the edges of the canvas as required. Trace and design on to the canvas with the waterproof, felt-tipped pen. If your design is coloured, it will be easy to trace on to the canvas; if not, outline the design in black and cover your working surface with a large piece of white paper—this makes tracing from an uncoloured design much easier.

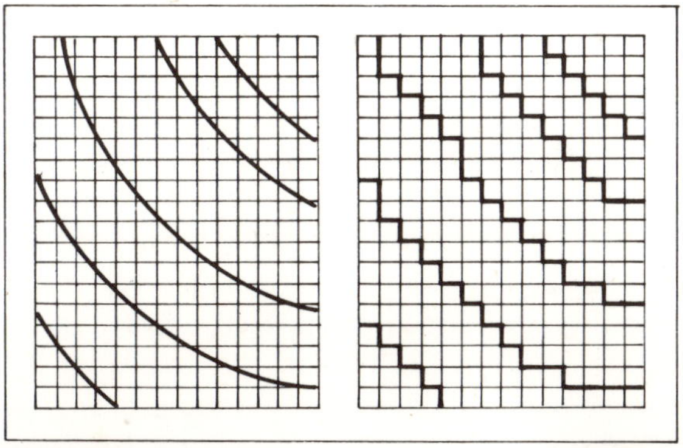

Fig. 4.5 Preparing a graph-paper guide. Original design lines left; graph-paper guide right.

Photo 4.6 This circular work, mounted on a square background, has been stitched on red linen, which shows through in places. The designer has used irregular thicknesses of wool and the Florentine (Bargello) stitch to show the theme of movement. Designed and stitched by Jean M. F. Carter.

Photo 4.7 Baby birds provided the inspiration for this design. Special interest is achieved by working the shapes in various materials, including raffia. Designed and stitched by Sister Catherine Cardis.

Next, paint the canvas. Although there are some people who will disagree, I think painting the canvas is essential. For one thing, a painted canvas ensures that any stitched canvas not fully covered by the wool is less conspicuous. Secondly, a painted canvas is a ready-made guide to the colours of the design. Even if you decide not to paint the canvas, write the colours in the appropriate spaces on the canvas or make a coloured tracing of the design. You can use wax crayons, indelible felt-tipped markers or acrylic paints to colour your canvas. As an extra precaution, test your indelible markers for waterproofness as described previously. Studio Magic Markers are readily available in art supply stores and come in a very wide range of colours. Acrylic paints are also sold in many colours and have only to be mixed with water. They are indelible when dry. If you are using these paints for the first time, be sparing with the amount and experiment with the consistency on a spare piece of canvas to be sure that the paint sits on top of the surface, rather than clogs the meshes (too much thick paint) or soaks and distorts the canvas (too much thin paint).

These suggestions for designing canvas embroidery pieces are not meant to be restricting, but rather to encourage the development of your own ideas. My philosophy about designing for yourself is to keep your mind open to any and all new ideas and never to stop experimenting. Please yourself and don't be limited by other people's taste. If you have an idea, try it. If that one doesn't work, it might give you an idea for another project. Experiment with different kinds of designs—floral, abstract, and animal—until you find the type of subject with which you feel most comfortable. Always keep your mind and eyes alive and your imagination alert, constantly exploring your surroundings for design inspirations.

5 Blocking and finishing canvas

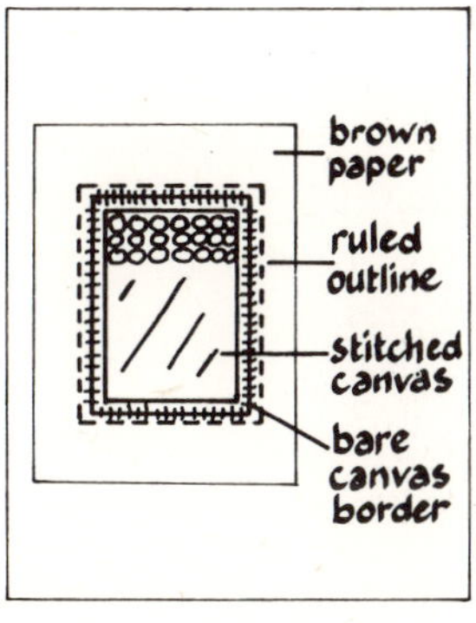

Fig. 5.1 Place the damp canvas, stitched side down, on the brown paper.

Blocking the Canvas

Almost without exception, no matter how uniform your tension, every canvas you stitch will be somewhat distorted and will need to be blocked. Blocking returns a piece to its original shape. You will witness the real professional touch in the smooth and even texture of your canvas after it has been blocked.

To block a canvas you will need the following items: a soft wooden surface slightly larger than the canvas, a sheet of brown paper, map pins (also called push pins), and water. Rule the size of the stitched canvas on the brown paper and cover the board with it. (Another method is to trace the outline of the canvas on to the brown paper before the canvas is stitched. However, occasionally, a piece of canvas is not perfectly straight and I believe ruling the dimensions is the most accurate method.) Wet the canvas by sprinkling it with water until it is quite damp but not sodden. Unless the piece has been worked in raised stitches, place the canvas, stitched side down, within the ruled outline marked on the paper (see Fig. 5.1). To preserve the fullness of raised stitches such as the twisted knot, but a soft towel between the brown paper and the canvas. Do not cover the markings on the paper because you will need them as a guide. Fasten the canvas to the board with the map pins, gently stretching and pulling the piece to fit into the outline marked on the paper. Begin by putting map pins in opposing corners and in the middle of each of the four sides; continue by halving the distance between each map pin until they are approximately 1-inch apart around the entire perimeter of the canvas. Do not put the map pins into the stitched canvas, but stick them along the 2-inch border of bare canvas. (If you are blocking a canvas with a finished edge, remember that you can only put map pins along three edges of the canvas; you must not stick map pins

Photo 5.1 This scene of everyday life was designed and stitched by N. Dowling.

in the finished edge, because they will leave holes in the stitching.) Having put in all the map pins, check that the canvas is perfectly square by placing the corner of a piece of paper over every corner of the canvas; adjust the canvas if it is not square. If your canvas is badly distorted, the stitches may continue to exert pressure on the canvas after it has been blocked; you will then have to block the canvas again until it holds its proper shape. Let the canvas dry out of the direct sun. The average drying time is approximately two days.

Small pieces that are not too distorted may be blocked by steaming. Pin the canvas—stitched side down—to the ironing-board cover with pins or tack it with map pins to the wooden board. Wet a pressing cloth and place it over the canvas. Heat the iron to 'steam' and carefully press the canvas, making certain not to put the full weight of the iron on the canvas. Keep the piece pinned to the ironing board cover until it dries. Drying time can be as short as a few hours or as long as a day and a half.

To guard against the canvas unravelling after it has been blocked and the

Photo 5.2 This circular panel was designed and stitched by Dr Wood.

masking tape (or fabric binding) trimmed, work a row of machine stitching around the perimeter of the canvas. To make the best use of the machine stitches, sew them as near as possible to the stitched canvas. Another way to prevent unravelling is to put a thin line of all-purpose glue along the last thread of each cut edge, especially those that you have cut within $\frac{1}{2}$ inch of the stitched canvas.

Assembling the Canvas

There are several ways to assemble and finish a canvas-embroidery project. Obviously, the most important factor is the function of the completed piece; this determines whether the canvas will be mounted, stitched to fabric or laced to a firm backing. Detailed instructions for making and finishing individual projects are given in Chapter 6; however, you should become acquainted with the three methods of joining stitched canvas—seaming, whipping and overlapping—so you can adapt them to your own projects.

Photo 5.3 This Bargello (Florentine) panel is from the collection at the Victoria & Albert Museum and was stitched around 1850. (Crown copyright, Victoria & Albert Museum).

Seaming

Provided that matching the meshes and the pattern is not important, seaming the stitched canvases is the most commonly used method of joining. After blocking, the two canvases can be treated as if they were fabric, i.e. with right sides together, stitch the seam. The seam allowance should be three stitched rows wide for fine canvas and two rows wide for coarse canvas; adjusting the seam allowance to the mesh size limits the bulk along the seam line. Trim the excess bare canvas to within $\frac{1}{2}$ to $1\frac{1}{2}$ inches of the seam, depending upon the nature of your project, cutting away the tape binding at the same time. Run a thin line of glue along the cut edges and let the glue dry. (See Fig. 5.2.) Press the seam open. To keep the unstitched seam allowance firmly in place, stitch it to the back of the piece with blind stitch.

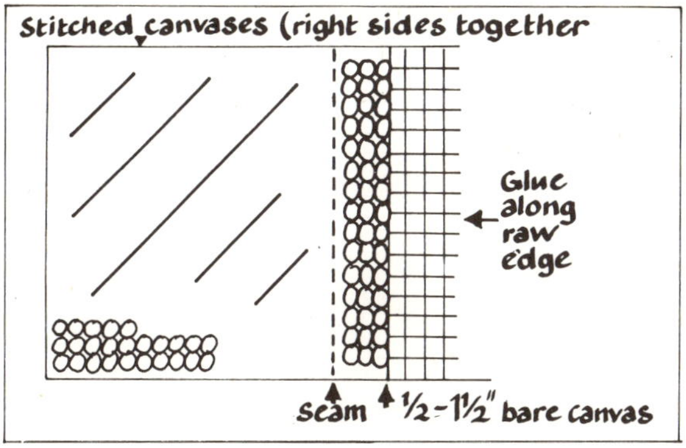

Fig. 5.2 Joining stitched canvas: seaming.

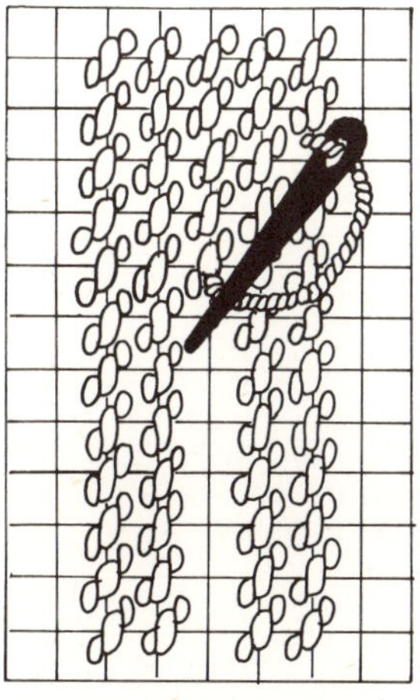

Fig. 5.3 Joining stitched canvas: whipping. Work a row of tent stitches over the whipped seam.

Whipping

Make a whipped seam when your project requires an almost invisible join at the front, but remember you cannot whip two pieces of stitched canvas unless the meshes are the same size. Whipping is, then, an excellent way to join cylindrical projects—pencil holders, napkin rings, and waste-paper baskets. When the two pieces have been blocked, trim off the excess bare canvas, leaving between $\frac{1}{2}$ and 1 inch; the tape binding will fall away as well. Glue the edges and let the canvas dry. Double under the remaining excess canvas along the edges to be joined, leaving one unworked thread along each edge. Match the two pieces of canvas, mesh to mesh, and whip the edges with heavy carpet thread. Work a vertical row of tent stitches over the whipping in the appropriate coloured yarn; it will be easier to stitch if you start at the top (See Fig. 5.3.) Blind-stitch the bare canvas to the back of the stitched canvas.

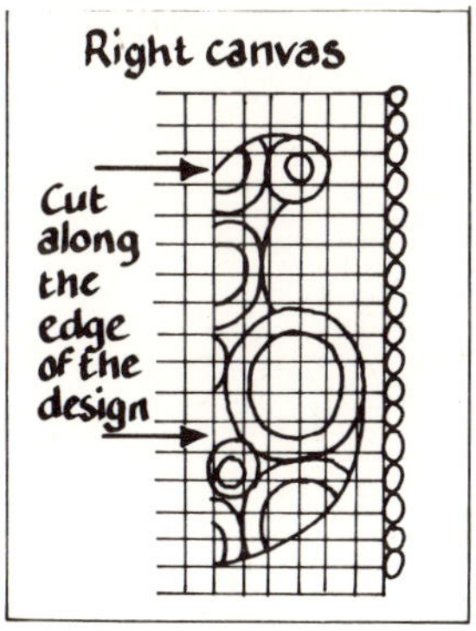

Fig. 5.4 Joining stitched canvas by overlapping. This is a useful method if the stitching is patterned elaborately. Stage one: trim the right-hand piece of canvas.

Overlapping

Overlapping two pieces of canvas is the least obtrusive way of joining and is a useful method if you are making a project so large that it must be worked in separate pieces; in addition, the pattern is uninterrupted from one piece to the next. Again, the pieces must have the same size meshes and should be blocked before they are joined.

Work your stitching on the right-hand canvas to within 2 inches of the intended edge. If you haven't already done so, outline the design in this 2-inch section. Trim the canvas exactly where the design stops (see Fig. 5.4). Glue this edge and let it dry. Stitch the left-hand canvas to within 2 inches of the edge of the design. If you haven't already done so, apply the design to this section of the canvas. Trim the bare canvas border to within five rows of the intended edge of the design (see Fig. 5.5). Glue the edges and let them dry. If the overlapping occurs in a section where there is no pattern, simply trim the glue both the right and left-hand piece as instructed above, ignoring the remarks about outlining the design.

Lay the right-hand canvas on top of the left-hand canvas, overlapping the

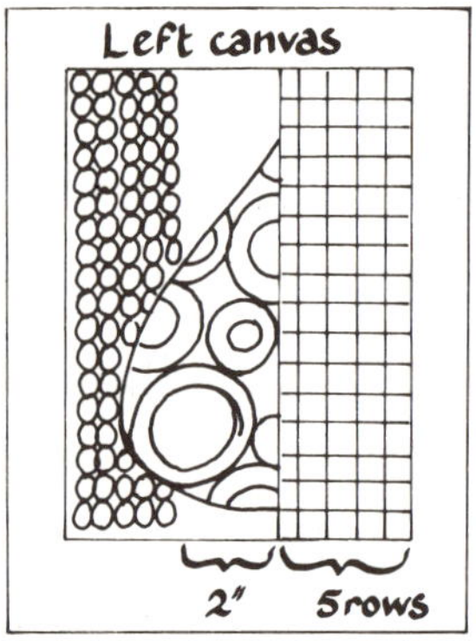

Fig. 5.5 Joining by overlapping. Stage two: trimming the left-hand piece of canvas.

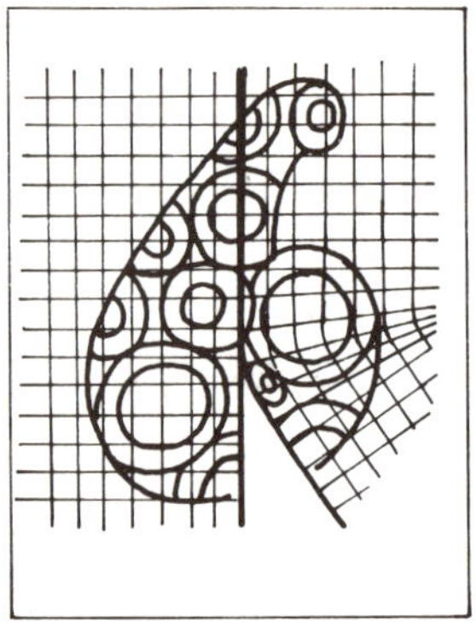

Fig. 5.6 Overlapping. Stage three: place the two pieces of canvas on top of one another, matching the bare meshes.

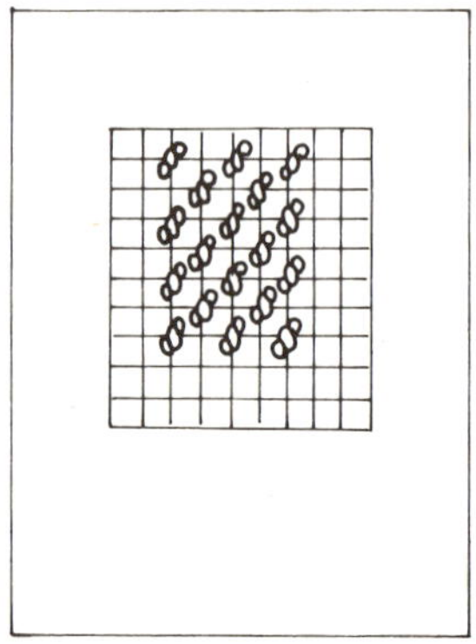

Fig. 5.7 Overlapping. Stage four: whip-stitch the two pieces of canvas together and then stitch them as though they were one piece of canvas.

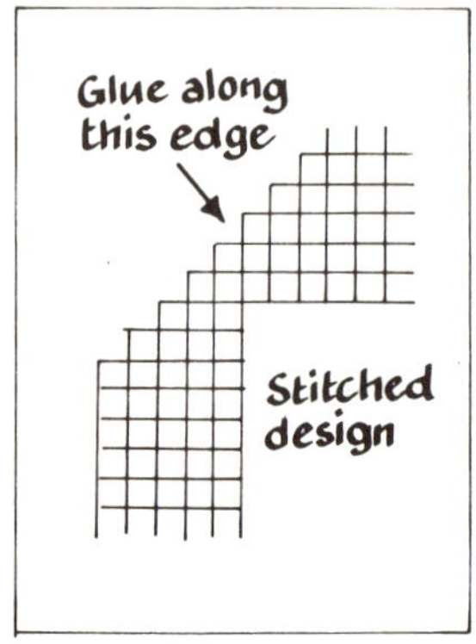

Fig. 5.8 To mitre a corner, first snip off along the diagonal and glue the edge.

five rows and matching the meshes (see Fig. 5.6). Whip-stitch the two pieces of canvas in place, covering alternate meshes, making two or three rows of stitches (see Fig. 5.7). Stitch the overlapped area as if it were one canvas.

Lacing and Mitring

Projects such as pictures and mirrors that require a rigid backing can be held in place by lacing. To ensure that there is a minimum amoung of bulk at the corners, mitre them; in fact, mitring is recommended for the corners of any project that should lie flat.

Before mitring the corners, you must first block your canvas. Then, begin by cutting away the bare-canvas border to within 1 inch of your stitching (the exact amount of canvas that is trimmed away will vary with the size of each project; large projects require a wider border of unstitched canvas). Snip off each corner on the diagonal to within roughly a $\frac{1}{2}$ inch of the stitching (Fig. 5.8). Put a thin line of glue along the cut edges and let the glue dry. At this point, if you were not lacing your piece, you would complete the mitring by turning under the diagonally cut edge to the corner point of your design (i.e., the remaining bare canvas and the finishing allowance) and then turn under the two adjoining sides and whip-stitch them together (Fig. 5.9).

However, when lacing a project, interrupt the mitring after the gluing step. Lay the trimmed and glued canvas right side down on a working surface and centre the backing board on it. Use heavy carpet thread and lace together the opposite sides of the canvas to within 3 inches of each corner, occasionally checking to be sure the canvas remains centred. Secure the

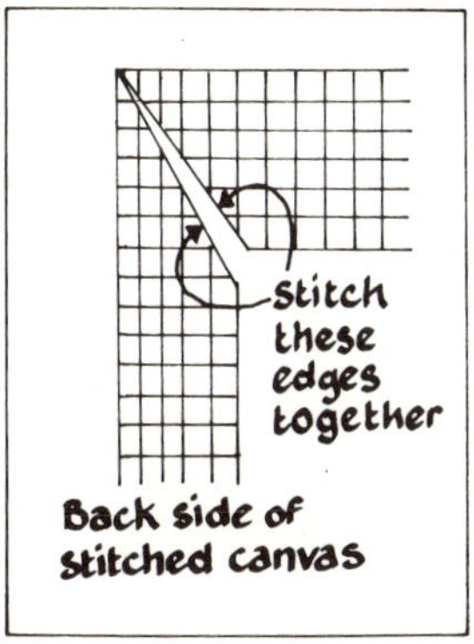

Fig. 5.9 Turn under the edges and whip-stitch them together to complete the corner.

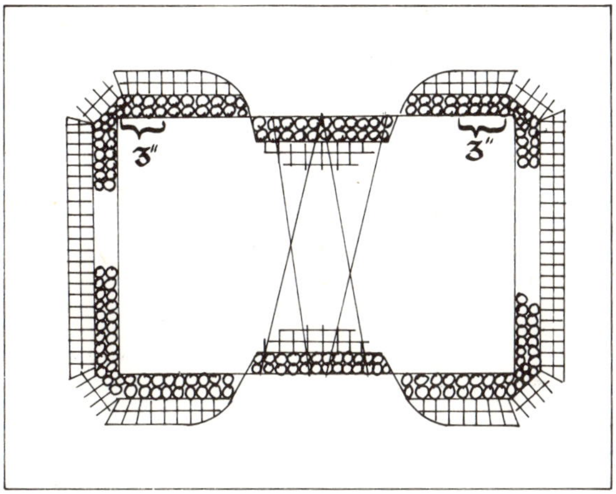

Fig. 5.10 Lacing canvas to a backing board.

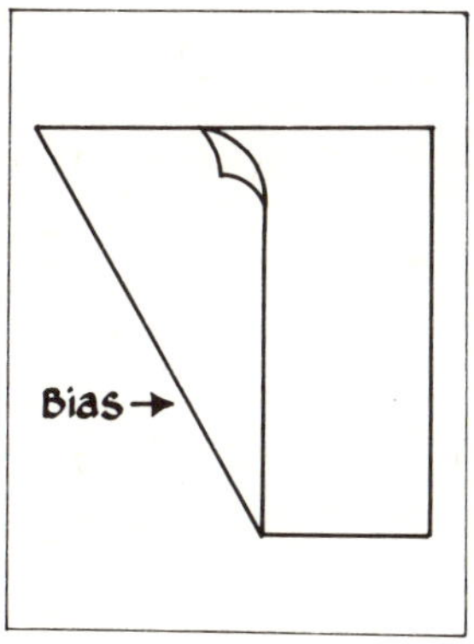

Fig. 5.11 Making welting. Stage one: finding true bias.

backing board firmly by lacing close to the edge of the board rather than close to the edge of the bare canvas border (see Fig. 5.10). Now complete the mitring by folding back each corner and whipping the adjoining sides together. Finish lacing the canvas. If you want to cover the lacing, glue or stitch a lining to the back of the board.

Finishing Touches

Yet another touch may be added to your project with the addition of a trimming. There are various edgings, braids, fringes and cordings available commercially; nonetheless, they may not be exactly the right colour. You can make your own trimming from the left-over wool or backing fabric: welting, cording, tassels and fringe are quite simple to make.

Welting

Welting is sewn to the finished canvas before the project is backed; it is made of long strips of fabric cut on the bias, stitched together and stuffed with cording. To begin, find the bias of the fabric by folding one corner of the piece so that the lengthwise and crosswise threads are matched (see Fig. 5.11). Crease the fold and cut away the corner along the crease; then measuring from the edge of the fabric, cut bias strips $1\frac{1}{2}$ inches wide (see Fig. 5.12). If you do not cut this fabric on the true bias, it will stretch out of shape. Join the bias strips together in one long piece to the length you require, as shown in Fig. 5.13. Buy some cording to put inside the welting. With the bias strip right side down, lay the cording in the centre and fold the bias strip over the cording, covering it. Matching the edges of the bias

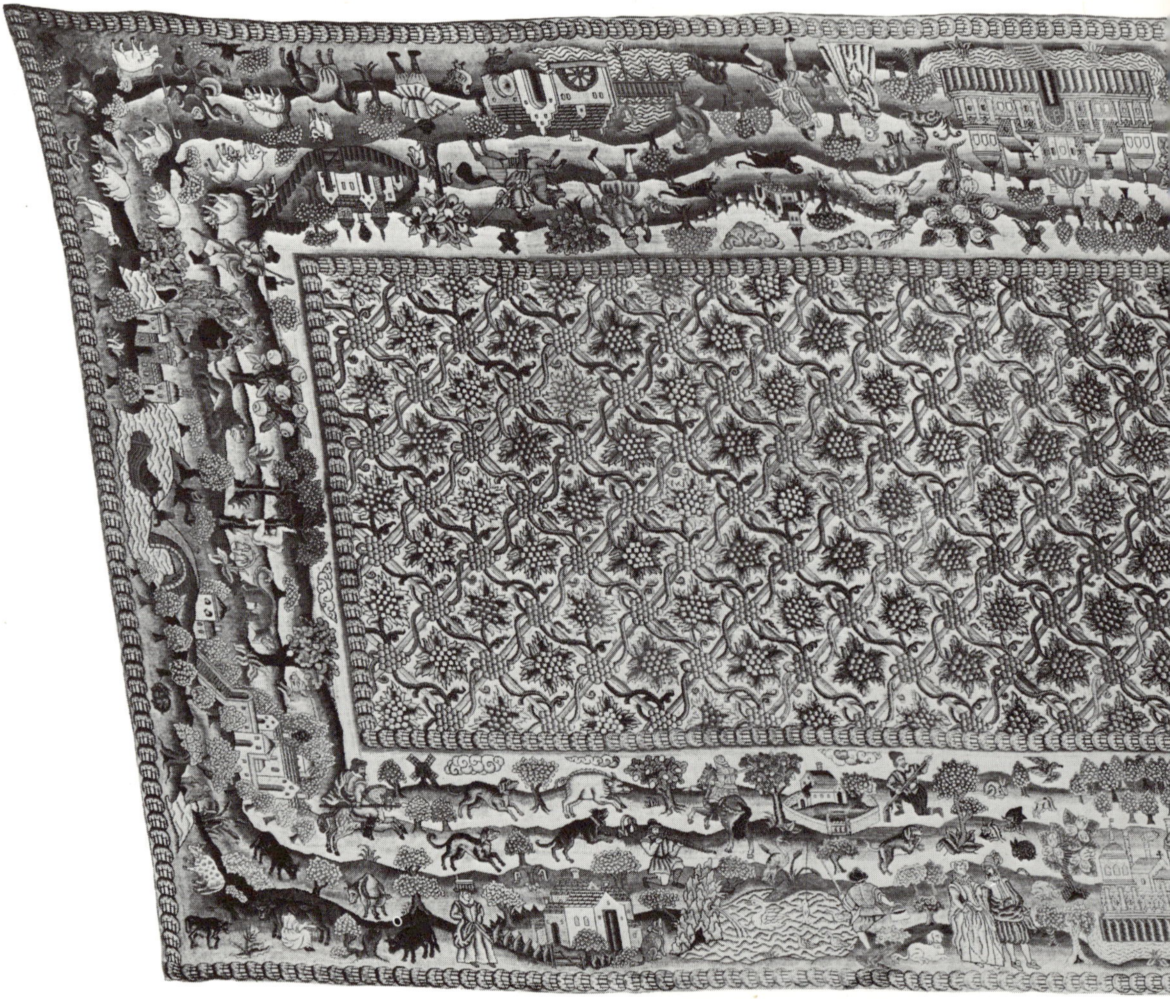

Photo 5.4 Stitched with silk on linen canvas, this Elizabethan table cover measures 13 feet long by 5 feet 9 inches wide. (Crown copyright, Victoria & Albert Museum).

Photo 5.5 Bargello has been incorporated into the design of this panel. Note the stitched frame. Designed and worked by Gill Davies.

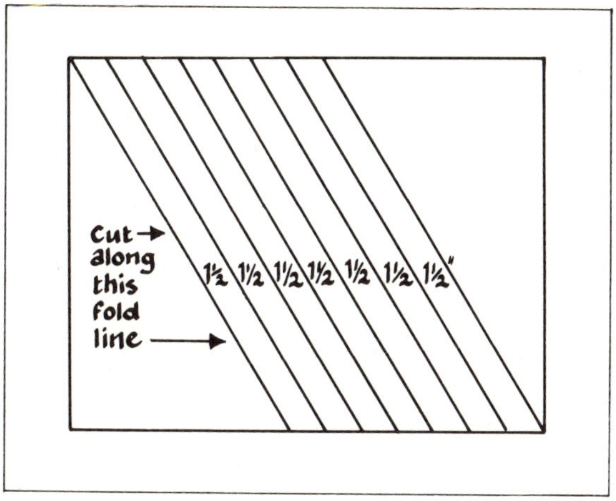

Fig. 5.12 Making welting. Stage two: cutting the strips.

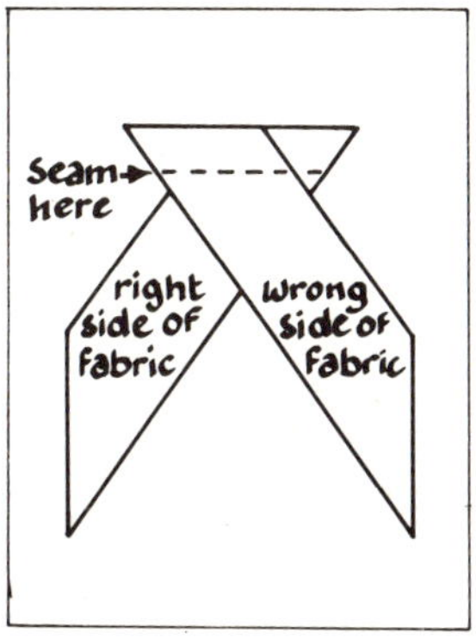

Fig. 5.13 Making welting. Stage three: joining the strips.

Fig. 5.14 Putting the cording inside the welting.

strip, run a seam along the cording, using the zipper foot of your sewing machine or very small hand stitches (see Fig. 5.14).

To stitch the welting to the canvas, put the blocked canvas, right side up, on the working surface. Lay the welting with the raw edge towards the bare canvas border, along the proposed seam line of the project and baste it along the seam line of the welting. When you are certain that the welting is in place, machine or hand-stitch it over the basting. Lay the backing fabric right side down on the canvas and welting and pin the seam. Baste along the seam line of the welting and machine or hand-stitch firmly.

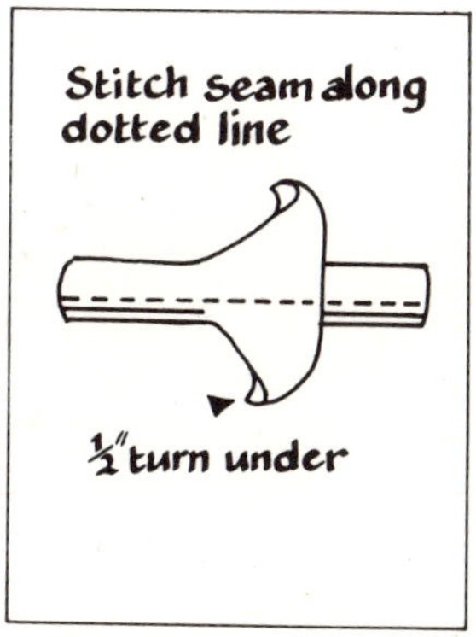

Fig. 5.15 Joining the two ends for continuous welting.

When you are making a project, such as a cushion, that requires continuous welting, you will have to join the two ends. To do this, open the last inch of one end of the welting seam and cut off 1 inch of cording. Turn one ½-inch of this raw edge to the inside and fit this turned under edge over the other end of welting. Seam the two pieces together. (See Fig. 5.15.) To make this join before stitching the welting to the canvas demands extremely accurate measurements; by far the most convenient method is to join the two ends of welting while you stitch the welting to the canvas. Stop and prepare the welting for the join a few inches before the meeting point.

Twisted Cording

Twisted cording is another trimming stitched on to the project after it has been seamed. Rather than being sewn into the seam, as with welting, twisted cording is stitched on top of the seam. It takes two people to make cording in what may seem to be a rather oldfashioned method; they should stand three times the desired length of the cording apart, each holding a pencil. Take a very long piece of wool and tie one end to the first pencil, then loop the wool back and forth between the pencils until you have as many strands as you need for the thickness of your cording. The two people should now stand far enough apart to taughten the yarn. Each then grasps the wool about 1 inch from the pencil with one hand and twists the pencil

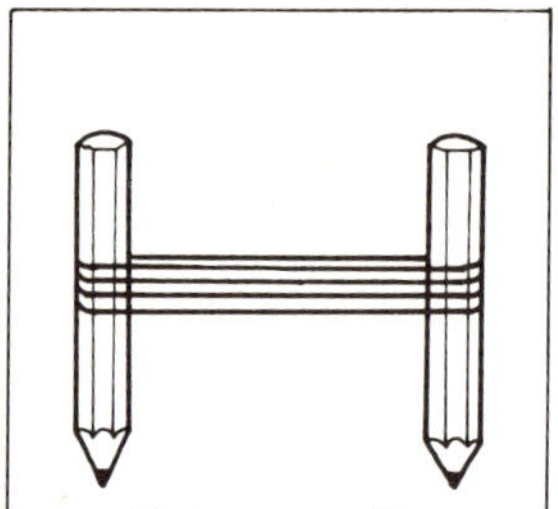

Fig. 5.16 Twisted cording: looping the wool round the pencils.

with the other hand. The pencils should be twisted in opposite directions (see Fig. 5.16). The wool will gradually shorten. When it begins to kink, keeping it taut, loop the yarn over a door knob and give both pencils to one person. The other person takes the centre of the yarn from the door knob and twists both strands together while carefully sliding one hand along the wool, releasing it at short intervals. (See Fig. 5.17.) Slide the fully twisted cording off the pencils and blind-stitch it in place.

Fringes

If you would like to make a fringe around the edges of your project, there are two ways of doing this. One method is to work a row of the turkey tufting stitch (instructions on page 75) between the very last row of your design and the first row of the finishing allowance (see Fig. 5.18). If the turkey tufting gets entangled in your wool as you stitch the finishing allowance, temporarily tape it to the front of the canvas.

The second way to fringe a project is only suitable for projects with a finished edge and requires a crochet hook that will fit between the meshes of the canvas. Cut the wool into strands that are twice the desired length of the fringe. Fold the strands in half and pass the crochet hook through the edge mesh from the front to the back in the exact spot where you want the fringe. Put a folded strand of wool on the end of the hook and pull it halfway through the canvas, forming a loop (see Fig. 5.19). Put the ends of the strand through the loop and pull them to tighten the fringe. Repeat the process between every mesh. If you want a thicker fringe, use more than one strand of wool and work the strands as if they were one. For an interesting effect, longer fringe may be knotted after it is made. Tie one strand from one fringe to one strand from the adjacent fringe as pictured in Fig. 5.20.

Tassels

Tassels sewn in the corner seams can be used alone or with welting and twisted cording. Cut about eight 36-inch lengths of yarn and two 9-inch lengths, you can use wool that is all the same or of different colours. (If you want a fatter or a thinner tassel, adjust the number of 36-inch strands.) Gather all the strands together in a bunch, lining up the ends. Fold the wool bunch in half twice and cut the folds at both ends. The strands should be 9 inches long. Tie this bunch together in the centre with one of the already cut 9-inch lengths—for decoration, tie six or eight loose reef (or square) knots in this length. Fold the bunch in half again so that the 9-inch length is at the top of the tassel which now measures $4\frac{1}{2}$ inches. Tie a second 9-inch length around the tassel approximately one third of the way from the top and make a few extra knots to be certain it is secure. If required, trim the tassel so that the ends are even. When pinning the seams of your project, simply pin the tassel in place in the corner and stitch the end into the seam.

Fig. 5.17 Twisting the strands of cording together.

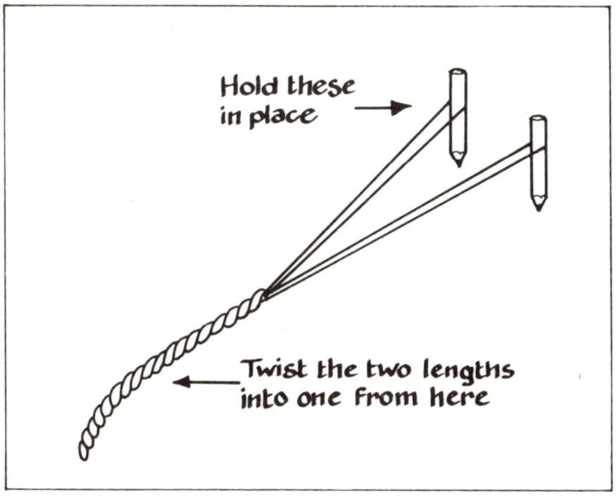

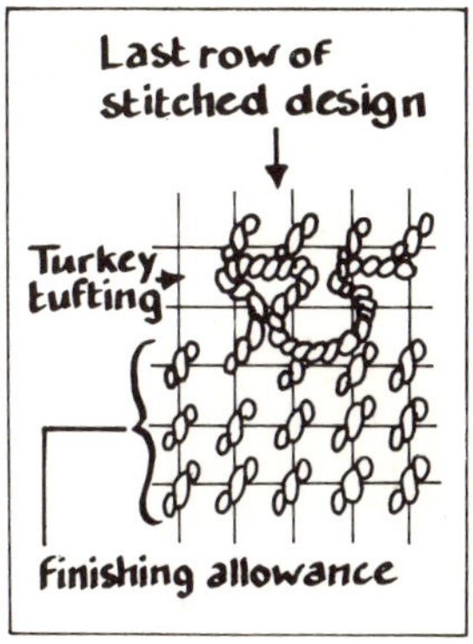

Fig. 5.18 Turkey tufting used as a finish.

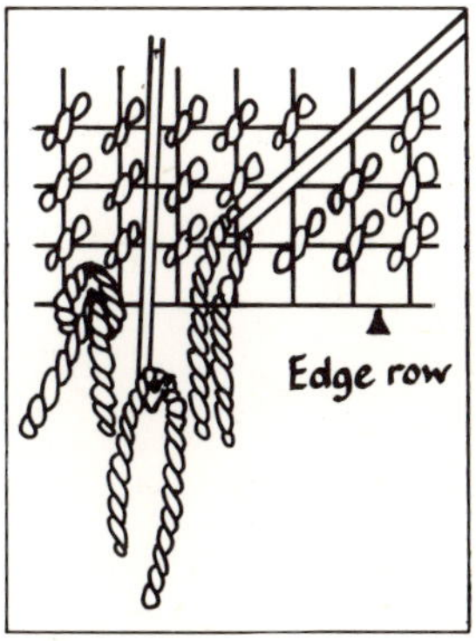

Fig. 5.19 Using a crochet hook to make a fringe finish.

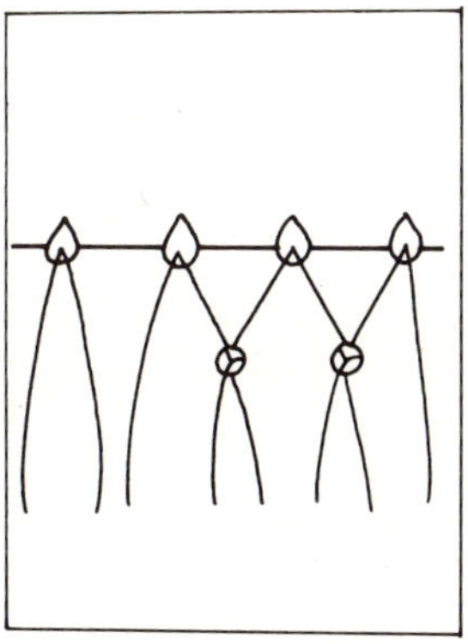

Fig. 5.20 Knotting the fringe makes an interesting finish and is not difficult to do.

You should now be able to back, mount and finish almost every project you want to stitch. Simple treat a stitched canvas as if it were very heavy fabric and you will have no trouble.

6 Projects

The projects you create with canvas embroidery are limited only by your imagination. Embroiderers have moved beyond the traditional cushions, pictures, and firescreens to fashionable shoulder bags and belts. Today the mode is to put part of your personality into what you make; something original is something special to be admired and preserved. Making something with your hands stirs up creative thoughts and the more you work canvas, the more familiar you will become with its versatility. You can wear it, you can decorate with it, you can give it as presents, you can use it as a covering for almost anything, and you can make ornaments for your Christmas tree with it. Keep experimenting and exploring.

The projects described in this chapter are only a representative sample of the things you can make. Some, such as the cushion and chair cover, are very traditional, but others—making insets in clothes and soft sculpture—are newer. Hopefully, they will all inspire some ideas of your own. Think about stitching a book marker, a book cover, an address book, a birthday card, matching desk accessories such as a pencil holder, letter holder and blotter ends, or a lamp shade, a spectacle case, a hair band, a watch band, a door stop (cover a brick with canvas embroidery), an evening bag, a shoulder bag, slippers, a pin cushion, a piano-bench cover, stair treads, a hassock, drapery pelmets (or valances), drapery tie-backs, luggage-rack straps, director's chair, card-table cover, napkin rings, games boards (such as chess or backgammon—see photo 6.1), drink mats, a waste-paper basket, a tennis-racket or squash-racket cover, a wallet, a tea-cosy, a toaster or mixer cover, a typewriter cover, a paperweight, insets for wooden boxes (photo 6.2), a bell-pull, a lavatory-seat cover, or even a pocket as point of emphasis for a long skirt or jeans.

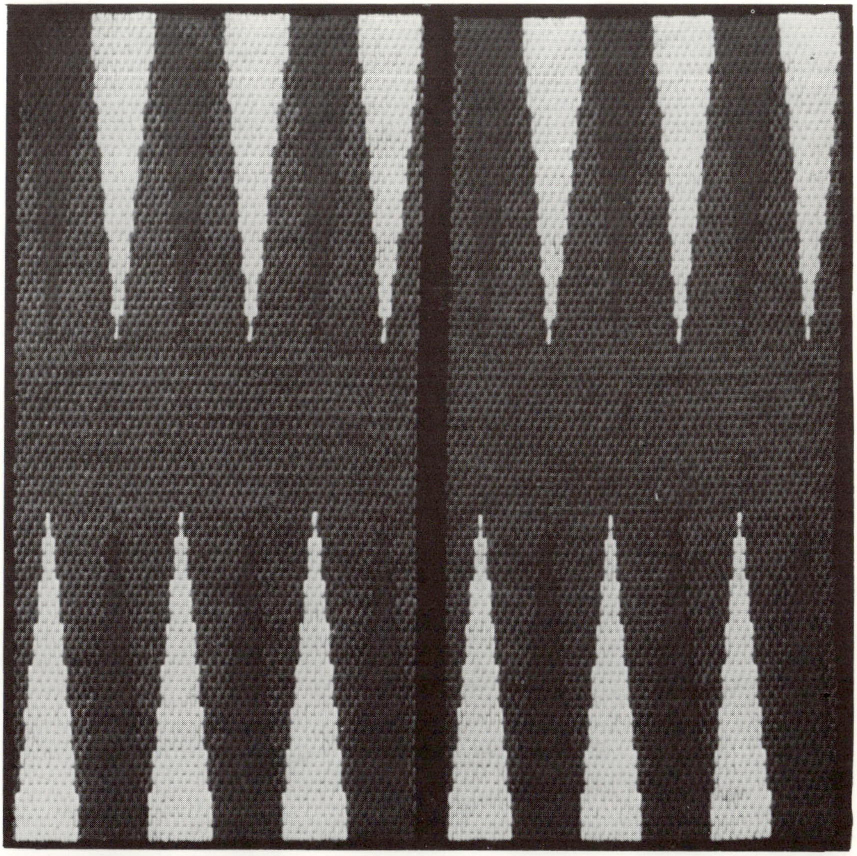

Photo 6.1 A game board is a useful project; this one was designed and worked by Bernard Taylor. (Courtesy of Womancraft *magazine)*

Photo 6.2 Another original use of the craft, both the box and the canvas work were designed and made by Bernard Berthon.

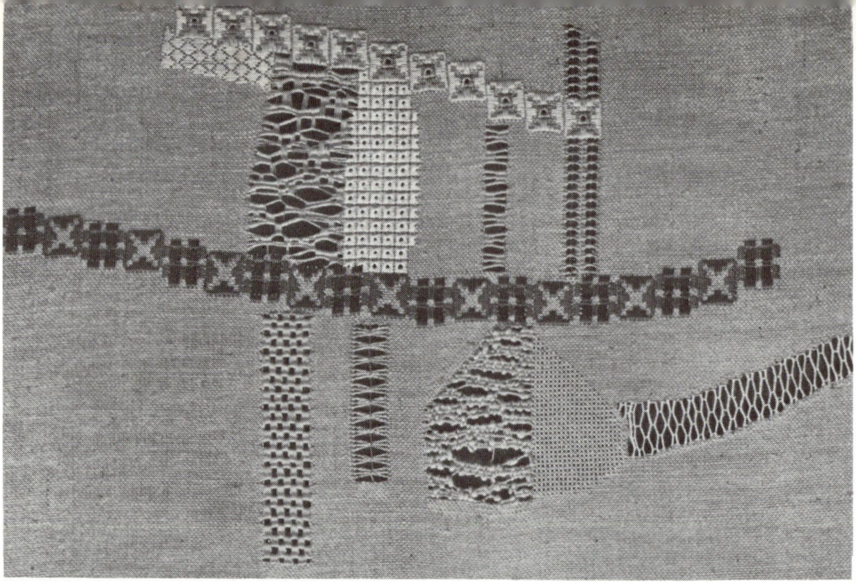

Photo 6.3 This design has combined canvas-embroidery stitches with pulled-threadwork; it is stitched on fine beige linen. Designed and worked by Maureen Phillips.

Cushion

One of the most traditional canvas-embroidery projects is a cushion. Today, they have become a decorator's fancy, of little practical use, but before the invention of upholstery, cushions were an absolute necessity for comfort. Try making one of unconventional shape rather than the usual 12- or 14-inch squares—possibly a giant one for sitting on the floor or a long, narrow one for a chair; or make a series of small cushions of different sizes to be displayed together in one corner of the sofa or on the bed. For stuffing, use kapok or Teryco, which are often sold in bulk, or buy a foam-rubber cushion form. If you use a ready-made form, remember that these are sold in specific dimensions and the size of your cushion will be determined by the dimensions of the form.

1. Select a design, dimensions, colouring, and stitches.
2. Cut the canvas, remembering to include three extra rows on each side and the 2 inches of bare canvas border as explained in Chapter 4. Prepare the canvas for stitching.
3. Stitch the piece and block it.
4. Make a row of machine stitches around the edge of the stitched canvas. If you are using a trimming, make this and stitch it in place as instructed in Chapter 5.
5. Cut a backing fabric to fit the canvas and pin it to the canvas on all sides, leaving a middle opening of about 10 inches, on one side, for an average-sized cushion. (The size of this opening will vary with the size of the cushion.)
6. Baste and then seam the two together.
7. Cut the excess canvas border and backing to within 1 inch of the seam on all sides. Diagonally trim the corners an additional $\frac{1}{2}$-inch.
8. To prevent the canvas from unravelling, run a line of glue along the cut edge as described in Chapter 5. Let the glue dry.

9. For the most satisfactory finish, you should make an inner cushion for the stuffing. The dimensions of the inner cushion should be exactly the same as those of the canvas cushion. Add seam allowance on all four sides and cut the inner cushion from any light-weight fabric such as muslin or cotton. With right sides together, seam the sides, leaving an 8-inch opening on the fourth side. Trim the seam allowance to $\frac{1}{4}$-inch; diagonally trim the corners. Turn the inner cushion inside out and stuff, making certain you get the stuffing well into each corner. Blind-stitch the opening to close.

10. Turn the stitched cushion inside out and insert the inner cushion. Turn the fabric along the opening to the inside and blind-stitch to close.

Chair Cover

Traditionally, dining-room chairs were covered in canvas embroidery and this is still a stunning way to make your work functional (photo 6.4). Try doing all the chairs in the same colours, but in different patterns, rather than using the same design for each chair. Or experiment with different types of chairs that are suitable for canvas embroidery, such as a piano stool, footstools, and foam chairs.

1. The first step is to make a pattern for the seat. Cut a piece of tissue paper or brown wrapping paper large enough to cover the edges of the seat.

Photo 6.4 Stitching canvas for the back and arms as well as the seat of this child's antique chair was the idea of Mrs H. Sale.

Put it over the seat and smooth it over the edges. Draw the outline and make sure that you have included the height of the seat as well. Alternatively, use the old seat cover.

2. Cut the canvas to the proper size, adding 1 inch on each of the four sides for finishing allowance.

3. Mark the outline on the canvas, bind the edges, and prepare the canvas for stitching.

4. Stitch the canvas and block it.

5. Make a row of machine stitches around the edges of the canvas. It is not necessary to trim away the excess canvas.

6. Unscrew the screws and remove the old seat from the chair. Remove the old upholstery tacks and the old seat cover.

7. Lay the needlework, face down, on a table or the floor and place the seat form, padding side down, on the stitched canvas. Centre the seat form on the canvas.

8. Fold the two sides of the canvas to the back of the seat form, pulling the canvas tight, but be careful not to pull the canvas too hard or you will move the form off centre. Make certain that you have pulled the canvas evenly on both sides and then hammer a tack in the centre of each. Continue to check for uniform tautness, and tack the sides every inch or two until you reach the corners.

9. Fold the two remaining sides of the canvas over the seat form and pull them tight, making sure they are pulled as tight as the other two sides. Put a tack in the centre of each of these sides and then work towards the corners, putting in a tack every inch or two, as you did previously. When you reach the corners, gently ease the canvas so that it lies flat and smooth. (If you prefer, you can mitre the corners before you begin tacking the canvas. Instructions for this appear in Chapter 5.)

10. For an extra finishing touch, and as protection from dust, cut a lining to fit the underside of the chair seat, allowing for a $\frac{3}{8}$ to $\frac{5}{8}$ of an inch seam allowance on all sides. Press under the seam allowance and tack it to the seat around the edges. If you use felt, cut the lining to the exact dimensions of the seat (you won't need to turn under the edges) and glue or tack it in place.

Note: The principles that apply when upholstering a chair seat apply also when mounting a canvas on a piece of wood for hanging. If the picture is to be framed, add an extra $\frac{1}{2}$ inch around the design as a finishing edge; this will fit under the edge of the frame. If you are not going to frame the canvas, work one or two rows around the design (depending on the thickness of the mounting board and the size of the canvas mesh), to cover the raw edges of the backing board. Cut the backing board to the exact measurements of the design. In this case, you should trim the excess canvas to within 1-inch of the stitched canvas and diagonally trim the corners to within a $\frac{1}{2}$-inch. Centre the canvas and tack it to the board. Either $\frac{1}{4}$-inch plywood or chipboard is excellent for the backing board.

Photo 6.5 The introduction of various materials besides wool and the use of stitches such as turkey tufting have given this wall hanging extra dimension. Designed and worked by Sue Singer.

Wall Hanging

A wall hanging is not put in a frame, but hangs free on the wall. Ordinarily, the hanging is attached to a rod, either directly and hung by a length of cording or strung through curtain rings. It will have to be lined. There is no limit to the shape and size of the hanging; you may even want to attach it to a bell-pull, but if you do decide to do this be certain to purchase your hardware first and stitch the canvas to the exact width required.

1. Select the dimensions of your wall hanging. You will not need any finishing allowance, so mark the exact dimensions on the canvas and cut. Bind the edges and prepare the canvas for stitching.
2. Stitch and block the canvas.
3. Trim the excess canvas to within 1-inch of the stitching and diagonally trim the corners to within a $\frac{1}{2}$-inch of the stitching. Run a thin line of glue around the edges and let it dry.

4. Turn under the excess canvas and whip-stitch it to the back.

5. Cut a lining to fit the hanging. If you are using a fabric that will fray, add a $\frac{1}{2}$-inch seam allowance. Press the seam allowance to the back of the lining and blind-stitch the front side of the lining to the canvas. If you are using felt and the raw edges will not fray, simply cut the lining to the exact dimensions of the hanging and blind-stitch it in place.

6. If you are using curtain rings, evenly space and stitch the curtain rings along the top edge of the lining and run the rod through the rings. For variety, you can blind-stitch two lengths of cording along the sides of the wall hanging.

7. To hang the canvas directly from the rod, cut another piece of lining the width of your hanging and 2 inches long. Add a $\frac{1}{2}$-inch seam allowance on all sides unless you are using felt, in which case the seam allowance is unnecessary.

Press the seam allowance to the back of the lining and stitch it in place. Stitch the strip along the top edge of the lining, leaving both sides open. Cut the rod to the appropriate length and insert it through the passageway. If you prefer, you can cut the rod a few inches longer and wrap a length of cording around the ends for hanging.

Insets in Clothing

One of the more modern ways of using canvas embroidery is in clothing—not only the usual waistcoat (or vest), but also as insets in dresses, jackets and trousers. The easiest way to begin is to buy a commercial pattern, rather than designing and making the pattern yourself, but of course, if you would rather do this, go right ahead. It is best to use a pattern with an inset that lies flat on all four sides; gathering a stitched canvas around the waist, for example, would be very uncomfortable and bulky. While it is possible to make darts, they do break up the design and add extra bulk. In selecting the fabric for the project, choose a heavy material that will support the weight of the canvas embroidery, such as velvet, corduroy or wool.

Note: For the example, I have selected a dress pattern with a flat inset in the front, and velvet fabric.

1. After purchasing the commercial pattern, separate the piece you plan to stitch in canvas embroidery from the rest. Trace its outline on to a piece of drawing paper but do not include the $\frac{5}{8}$-inch seam allowance, as indicated in the pattern. (Put the drawing paper against a window to make it transparent.)

2. Trace the design within this outline; colour it and select your stitches.

3. Adding three additional rows of canvas for seam allowance on all

sides, and the usual 2-inch border of bare canvas, measure a rectangle in which the paper pattern fits. Cut a piece of canvas this size and bind the edges.

4. Transfer the outline of the pattern to the canvas. Prepare it for stitching.

5. Stitch the canvas and block it.

6. Run a row of machine stitching around the edges of the canvas embroidery and trim away the excess canvas to within $\frac{1}{2}$-inch of the stitching. Diagonally trim any corners. Run a thin line of glue around the raw edges of the canvas and let this dry.

7. Assemble your project as you would normally, treating the stitched canvas as if it were a piece of fabric. To assure a minimum of bulk, open all the canvas seams and whip them to the back of the stitched canvas. You may also blind-stitch a lining to the inside of the canvas.

Photo 6.6 Stitched in varying shades of dark brown and rust, this piece combines two crafts: canvas embroidery and appliqué. (Designed and stitched by Pat Bean)

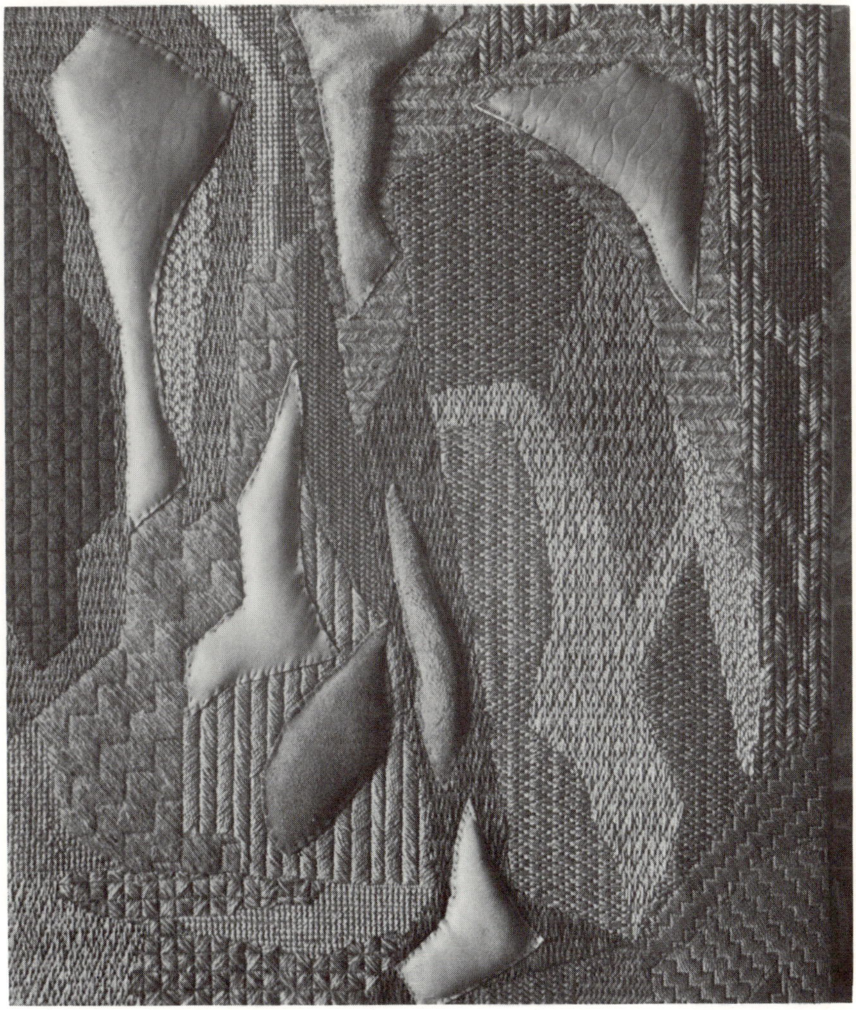

Photo 6.7 This Bargello (Florentine) stitched bag is another style of handbag adaptable to canvas embroidery. Designed and stitched by Miss N. Dowling.

Carrier Bag (shopping bag)

In the past few years, carrier bags or shopping bags have become an integral part of fashion. Originally, they were made of plastic or paper, but now they are made from durable fabrics and canvas embroidery. If you make and use this type of bag, you are also saving a few trees and the environment as well.

1. Select the dimensions and shape of your bag. It could have square or rounded corners, either both or one side stitched on canvas, a stitched or fabric gusset (or no gusset at all), or long or short handles. The example is 13 × 15 in., has one stitched side and a fabric gusset.
2. Mark the dimensions and shape on a piece of drawing paper and transfer your design. Choose the colour scheme and stitches. If you want to stitch a gusset, determine its length by adding the width and two lengths of the bag together. For example, in the sample, the gusset would be 43 inches long (13 plus 15 plus 15).
3. Cut the canvas, adding three rows of canvas on three sides and the usual 2-inch border of bare canvas. Prepare the top edge for a finished edge

as described in Chapter 5.

4. Bind the edges, and prepare the canvas as you wish for stitching.

5. Stitch the canvas and block it.

6. Run a row of machining close to the edges of the canvas embroidery and trim the bare canvas to within ½-inch of the stitching. Diagonally trim the corners. Glue the raw edges and let the glue dry.

7. With the right sides together, pin the front panel of the bag to one side of the gusset. Stitch the seam. Repeat this step for the back of the bag, whether it is stitched canvas or fabric. Clip the rounded corners, if you have them, so they will lie flat.

8. Make handles—either from cording or by stitching a long strips of fabric together on three sides, turning it right side out and blind-stitching the open end. Attach at least 3-inches of each handle to the inside of each side panel of the bag.

9. Cut a lining for the bag, not forgetting to include a gusset-seam allowance on all four sides. Press the seam allowance to the back along the top edge. Stitch the seams of the lining.

10. Pin the lining to the inside of the bag and blind-stitch in place.

Hat-band or Belt

With the advent (or rather return) of the wide-brimmed floppy hat, there has grown an interest in original hat-bands. A canvas-embroidered hat band is attractive and easily made by lining a length of stitched canvas with gros-grain ribbon and leaving some extra ribbon at either end to tie in a bow. Or you could fit the band to the crown of the hat and whip the ends together. A belt is made by the same principle. For a belt with a single-buckle closing, add about 6-inches to the waist size; for a double-buckle closing, deduct the width of the buckle from the waist size, and add 2-inches for securing the buckles in place. Small projects such as these (and those shown in photo 6.8) can be made with more detailed designs if they are stitched on the finer canvases.

1. Determine the finishing technique, and the dimensions of your project. If you are using gros-grain ribbon to finish your hat-band or belt, remember to check the width in which the ribbon is available and make your project exactly that width. To keep the bulk to a minimum, in both projects, do not add any finishing allowance, just the usual 2-inch, bare-canvas border.

2. Cut the canvas and bind the edges.

3. Transfer the dimensions of the belt or hat-band to the canvas and prepare for stitching.

4. Stitch and block the canvas.

5. For both projects, run a row of machine stitching around the edges of

Photo 6.8 This evening bag is an ideal project for canvas embroidery, as is the accompanying needle case. The bag was designed and worked by Joanne Graham; the needle case by Mrs Howard Jones.

the stitched canvas. Trim the bare-canvas border to within ½-inch of the stitching and diagonally trim the corners. Whip-stitch the bare canvas to the back of the stitched canvas.

6. To finish the hat-band, centre the canvas embroidery on an appropriate length of gros-grain ribbon and blind-stitch in place; or, if you have tailored the band to the hat, whip the two ends together as described in Chapter 5.

7. To finish the belt, cut a lining from a non-slip material such as felt, velvet (you may be able to buy a remnant) or suède, and blind-stitch it in place. Attach the buckles and fastenings.

Mirror Frame

Framing with canvas embroidery is an imaginative way to decorate a mirror; you could, for example, make an oversized frame for a small mirror. A small repeated design or a geometric design is usually recommended, but try designing a simple picture—clouds and trees, flowers, a row of houses—and incorporating the mirror as part of the design. Any shape or size of mirror will do, just be sure it is thin and has polished edges because it will be attached to the front of the canvas, in a space exactly its own size, that you will leave unstitched.

1. Select the dimensions of the mirror and the frame. Rule the mirror size on a piece of drawing paper, and fit the design of the frame around this shape.

2. Prepare the canvas for stitching, and transfer to it the design of the frame, including the empty space. Add two rows for finishing allowance because the stitched canvas will be laced to ¼-inch-thick backing board.

3. Stitch the canvas and block it.

4. Sew a row of machine stitches around the edges of the stitched canvas.

5. Trim away the binding and diagonally trim the corners to within 1-inch of the stitching. Glue these cut edges and let the glue dry.

6. Buy a piece of plywood or chipboard, $\frac{1}{4}$-inch thick, exactly the dimensions of your project, not including the two rows of finishing allowance.

7. Lace the stitched canvas to the backing board as described in Chapter 5. Cover the backing with a lining.

8. To attach the mirror, first put several strips of masking tape across the back of the mirror—especially if it does not have a backing that will adhere to glue. Use a very strong glue such as Araldite or Duco cement, and position the mirror in the blank canvas space. Pile some books or magazines on top of the mirror until the glue sets.

9. Screw two screws into the backing and string picture wire between them for hanging.

Waste-paper Basket

The technique used to assemble a waste-paper basket is the same as that used for a pencil holder, a letter holder and any other project that involves covering a circular form with canvas embroidery. (Actually this shape is one of the easiest to cover.) You can use an old waste-paper basket or any suitably sized, rigid tubular container. When you plan your design, remember that the two ends of the project will be whipped together and meet, so the design must match.

1. Select the container, measure the height of it and deduct 1 inch; this will be the height of your stitched canvas (the inch deducted will later be divided between the top and the bottom edges of the container and covered by ribbon or another trim). The width of the borders may be altered to suit your needs, by increasing the amount deducted from the height of the container, but remember that the figure must be evenly divisible by two. Measure the circumference (the distance around the outside of the container); this will be the width of your canvas.

2. Plan your design to fit within these dimensions. Prepare the two ends of the canvas for whipping (instructions in Chapter 5) and prepare the canvas for stitching.

3. Stitch and block the canvas.

4. Trim the excess bare canvas to within $\frac{1}{2}$-inch (or the width of your trim) of the stitching. Glue the raw edges and let them dry.

5. Whip the two ends (including the $\frac{1}{2}$-inch of bare canvas) together as described in Chapter 5.

6. Fit the canvas over the container. Glue $\frac{1}{2}$-inch-wide trimming or ribbon over the bare canvas.

7. If necessary, make a felt lining for the container and glue it in place.

Photo 6.9 This is another blending of Florentine (Bargello) work with canvas-embroidery stitches; the sections of bare canvas add interest. Designed and stitched by Janet Riden.

Stuffed Toys or Soft Sculpture

Making a stuffed toy is an original way of interpreting your three-dimensional ideas in canvas. However, stuffed toys need not be only for children—take the idea one step further and make some soft sculptures. Either project can be any shape, although smooth, flowing curves are easier to assemble than protruding points. The principles of making either a toy or soft sculpture are the same and the possibilities are countless. Make a peanut for a friend who adores peanuts, a single flower growing in a pot, a huge wedge of cheese or a large fried egg accompanied by separate slices of bacon, a giant bar of chocolate, a huge strawberry or even a mobile. If you want your project to stand upright, you must give it a base large enough to support it (if you prefer not to stitch this, it can be made of felt) and this should be weighted. The project itself is composed of two canvas-embroidered pieces stitched together with the same design on both.

1. Select the design and dimensions of your project. As a guide, if the base of your project is between 4 and 5 inches in diameter, the height should be between $8\frac{3}{4}$ and $9\frac{3}{4}$ inches and the width between 9 and 10 inches.

2. Prepare the canvas for stitching. The pieces of your project will be whipped together, so there is no seam allowance. Remember to cut the canvas in a square or rectangle, no matter what the shape of your project.

3. Stitch and block the canvases.

4. To minimise the bulk at the join, trim the bare canvas as close as possible to the stitching on three sides of the body pieces of the project. Trim the base edge of both these pieces to within $\frac{1}{2}$-inch of the stitching. Glue all raw edges and let the glue dry. Turn the $\frac{1}{2}$-inch of bare canvas around the base edges of both pieces to the inside and baste in place. Trim the base itself to within $\frac{1}{2}$-inch of the stitching. Glue the raw edge and let it dry.

5. With the unstitched sides of the canvas together, whip the two body pieces together, leaving the base edge and an opening along the top unstitched. (Detailed instructions for whipping appear in Chapter 5.) This opening will be used to insert and fit the base and for stuffing, so be sure it is large enough. To make the whipping as unnoticeable as possible, use the appropriate coloured wool, changing colours whenever necessary. Make loose whipping stitches so that the project will have some give when it is stuffed.

6. Make a tiny bag from some scrap material and insert some weights in it. Stitch the fourth side closed. Whip this to the centre of the inside of the base.

7. Insert the base through the top opening and fit it, stitched side downwards, to the base of the body of the project. Pin and then whip-stitch the base in place; don't worry about the untrimmed canvas inside.

8. Stuff the project with pieces of kapok, Teryco or old nylon hose and then use whip-stitch to close the top opening.

Note: If your project does not have a base, simply whip all three sides, work a row of canvas-embroidery stitching over the whipping if that is feasible, and stuff it through the opening in the top. Then, whip the opening closed.

Christmas Stocking

Another novel idea is to stitch a Christmas stocking. Some people feel it is a waste of time to spend so many hours making a project that will be used once a year, but what could be more cheery than a familiar decoration to help celebrate the holiday annually. You could plan a design that has a name across the top and a sprinkling of traditional holly leaves, Christmas bells, snowflakes, Christmas trees, and wreaths over the stocking or try adapting a folk design as has been done with the example shown in colour plates.

1. Select the dimensions for your stocking and sketch the shape and design on a piece of paper. (The example is 10 inches wide and 14½ inches in height.) Cut a rectangle of canvas on which to mark the outline of the stocking. Remembering to either keep the design inside the seam allowance or add ½-inch on three sides for this, prepare the canvas for stitching. If you choose, you may prepare the top edge of the stocking for a finished edge; see Chapter 5 for full instructions.

2. Stitch and block the canvas.

3. Cut a felt backing, also including seam allowances. The top edge of the lining will be even with the stitched canvas so you will not need a seam allowance there.

4. Run a line of machine stitching around the edges of the stitched canvas. Trim the excess bare canvas to within a ½-inch of the stitching and glue the raw edges. Let this dry. If you have not prepared the top for a finished edge, turn the bare canvas to the inside along this edge and stitch in place.

5. With right sides together, pin and then stitch the lining to the stitched canvas; you will probably have to clip the seams at the curve around the ankle to relieve the stress—make short clips perpendicular to the seam.

6. To hang the stocking, cut a strip of felt, fold it in half lengthwise and stitch it to the inside of the stocking.

Note: The same principles involved in making a Christmas stocking apply to any project that is shaped like an envelope; for example, a spectacle case.

I very much hope that this chapter—and the whole book, for that matter—gives you some inspiration for your own ideas. The thrill of making something that you have planned and then stitched with your own hands is a feeling that is very special. My most ardent advice is to experiment and let the ideas flow.

List of suppliers

A.N.I. Art Needlework Industries Ltd,
Ship Street,
Oxford

Mrs Mary Allen,
Turnditch,
Derbyshire

G. S. Arnold,
Butterley Street,
Leeds

Beecrafts,
77 Church Street,
Guisborough,
Yorkshire TS14 6BX

The Campden Needlecraft Centre,
High Street,
Chipping Campden,
Gloucestershire

Craftsmans Mart,
Broadlands Shortheath,
Farnham,
Surrey

Dryad,
Northgate,
Leicester

B. Francis,
4 Glentworth Street,
London NW1

Hugh Griffiths,
Brookdale,
Beckingham,
Bath,
Avon

Thomas Hunter,
36 Northumberland Street,
Newcastle

Jackson's Rug-Craft Centre,
Croft Mill,
Hebden Bridge,
Yorkshire HX7 8AP

The Ladieswork Society Ltd,
Delabere House,
Embroideries,
Morton-in-Marsh GL56 0AS

Luxury Needlepoint Tapestries,
36 Beauchamp Place,
London SW3

Mace & Nairn,
89 Crane Street,
Salisbury,
Wiltshire

Needlewoman Shop,
146 Regent Street,
London W1

Nottingham Handicraft Company Ltd,
Melton Road,
West Nottingham

Northern Handicrafts Ltd,
Belle Vue Mill,
Westgate,
Burnley BB11 15D

Christine Riley,
53 Barclay Street,
Kincardinshire AB3 2AR

Royal School of Needlework,
25 Princes Gate,
Kensington SW7 1QE

Seldon Tapestries Ltd,
10 Kings Mansions,
Lawrence Street,
London SW3

The Silver Thimble,
33 Gay Street,
Bath, Avon

Spinning Jenny,
Bradley,
Keighley,
Yorkshire BD20 9DD

Mrs Joan L. Trickett,
110 Marsden Road,
Burnley,
Lancashire

The Wool Shop and Home Artistic Ltd,
89/90 Darlington Street,
Wolverhampton,
Staffordshire

Yarns,
28 Upper East Hayes,
Bath BA1 6LP

Index